*Dedicated to Dawn Botkins for her tir
friend from childhood Aileen, until th
heart.*

Table of Contents

5. Life On The Road

- The Hippie Councilor (Aged 16)
- The Commune in Colorado
- Back in Michigan briefly (Aged 17)
- Back On The Road Again
- Her Brother Keith Dying In Hospital
- Married briefly in Orlando, Florida (Aged 20)
- Sex Work
- Other Jobs
- Alcoholism
- Getting Raped, Assaulted & Robbed
- 3rd Real Relationship
- Toni – 'My First Lezzy Encounter' (Aged 29)
- Relationship with Tyria Moore
- Living The Good Life
- Last Relationship After The Murders
- Final Words On Her Past

Pictures

Acknowledgments

Synopsis

A letter correspondence over many years between Aileen and her best friend from childhood Dawn was collated into a book, in the order the letters were sent.

Mixed into the letters were long essays about her life on the road which she asked Dawn to keep safe encase she ever wrote enough that she could start knocking it into an autobiography.

As I was reading it, I found her experiences of the time she lived through so fascinating that I wanted to save each one and see it in perspective to her other memories in the timeline of her life.

So that's what I've done here. And if it's useful in the future to anyone's creative pursuits, like writing non-fiction plays or graphic novels, essay reflections on her life, the 70s, or even fictional stories with characters based on Aileen, then all the better.

I first discovered Aileen's story through Nick Broomfield's documentary, 'The Life And Death Of A Serial Killer' which gave an in-depth look into the tortured childhood she came from.

The myopic reason it resonated with me is the very tenuous comparison I saw between myself and Aileen, in that she had been setting off hitchhiking and living on communes since the age of 15 with the hope of doing some psychological healing from the circle she was stuck moving in in Troy, Michigan, where she grew up.

And that this was a very romanticized road to take at the time, although I don't think Aileen bought into all of that, as she was simply homeless from the age of 13, and traveling further afield was a nice break from relying on friends in Troy. But, she loved the hippie music of the era and cherished every commune she stayed at for the people who attempted a new more compassionate way of relating to one another.

So for me, that was activist circles, and it left me with the understanding that you don't get a choice in the strange situational reasons that different people will be alienated from society enough to join this or that campaign, but you can make the best of the journey all the same.

I'll include a forward by Hunter S. Thompson on the hippie counter-culture for this reason anyway. Then the rest is almost all Aileen, with just a few excerpts from interviews in the documentary.

Finally here are Aileen's words on her attempts to write this autobiography from jail:

This is being done like Sound off. But of course like I said, real brief, hitting area's most important. Like looks and character, on Mom, Dad, Lori, Barry, Keith, then to me, and the life I lead. That's going to be really hard to be brief. Do you know how much I've seen?! Geez! But, I'll get through. And must, before I should die soon.

I am really close to God. Read the Bible three times all the way through. And even in my young and road days, I got into God (Jesus) and my heart was as good then it as it is now. Even though I became a pro in being a prostitute I still believed on the road anyway, and always willing to give a helping hand to anyone, even "strangers" because of my experiences from my young days and how I was treated. I cannot elaborate how many times sex was forced upon me, but when I do get some time down the road to get a book out. It is going to be about my life, not these crimes. And how people should NOT treat each other like this.

Disclaimers

Putting this together is not an endorsement of Aileen's views or actions, she was failed by society and as a result, was a danger to that society in return. And even though reading stories of her beating up a homophobe or escaping juvenile detention is heartwarming, the way in which she was a danger was by no means always good. She killed for money, was a hateful racist, a controlling abusive partner, and abused animals through neglect.

So, bear all that in mind when you're reading & obviously be very skeptical of whether some of the claimed facts & narratives are even true.

I'm not claiming to own the copyright or seeking to earn money from the original letters.

I grammar and spell corrected it, as Aileen was not very literate, it would have been a torturous read otherwise for many. But, if you want to see the letters preserved with their original spelling, you can simply read the book, Dear Dawn.

And if you're simply curious to cross-reference where a specific paragraph from a story fits into the original letter, you can copy a rare word or sentence, pull up an e-book of Dear Dawn, hit Ctrl+F, and paste to see.

Finally, I don't know what genre this would fall into, but I think it's fairly close to arriving at what her autobiography might have looked like, had she desired to or been mentally well enough to finish filling in key moments, with a ghostwriter to help. So, unfinished memoir or biography maybe? You decide.

Foreword – The Hippies by Hunter S. Thompson

The best year to be a hippie was 1965, but then there was not much to write about, because not much was happening in public and most of what was happening in private was illegal. The real year of the hippie was 1966, despite the lack of publicity, which in 1967 gave way to a nationwide avalanche in Look, Life, Time, Newsweek, the Atlantic, the New York Times, the Saturday Evening Post, and even the Aspen Illustrated News, which did a special issue on hippies in August of 1967 and made a record sale of all but 6 copies of a 3,500-copy press run.

But 1967 was not really a good year to be a hippie. It was a good year for salesmen and exhibitionists who called themselves hippies and gave colorful interviews for the benefit of the mass media, but serious hippies, with nothing to sell, found that they had little to gain and a lot to lose by becoming public figures. Many were harassed and arrested for no other reason than their sudden identification with a so-called cult of sex and drugs. The publicity rumble, which seemed like a joke at first, turned into a menacing landslide. So quite a few people who might have been called the original hippies in 1965 had dropped out of sight by the time hippies became a national fad in 1967.

Ten years earlier the Beat Generation went the same confusing route. From 1955 to about 1959 there were thousands of young people involved in a thriving bohemian subculture that was only an echo by the time the mass media picked it up in 1960. Jack Kerouac was the novelist of the Beat Generation in the same way that Ernest Hemingway was the novelist of the Lost Generation, and Kerouac's classic "beat" novel, On the Road, was published in 1957. Yet by the time Kerouac began appearing on television shows to explain the "thrust" of his book, the characters it was based on had already drifted off into limbo, to await their reincarnation as hippies some five years later. (The purest example of this was Neal Cassady, who served as a model for Dean Moriarty in On the Road and also for McMurphy in Ken Kesey's One Flew Over the Cuckoo's Nest.)

Publicity follows reality, but only up to the point where a new kind of reality, created by publicity, begins to emerge. So the hippie in 1967 was put in the strange position of being an anti-culture hero at the same time as he was also becoming a hot commercial property. His banner of alienation appeared to be planted in quicksand. The very society he was trying to drop out of began idealizing him. He was famous in a hazy kind of way that was not quite infamy but still colorfully ambivalent and vaguely disturbing.

Despite the mass media publicity, hippies still suffer or perhaps not from a lack of definition. The Random House Dictionary of the English Language was a best seller in 1966, the year of its publication, but it had no definition for "hippie." The closest it came was a definition of "hippy": "having big hips; a hippy girl." Its definition of "hip" was closer to contemporary usage. "Hip" is a slang word, said Random House, meaning "familiar with the latest ideas, styles, developments, etc.; informed, sophisticated, knowledgeable[?]." That question mark is a sneaky but meaningful piece of editorial comment.

Everyone seems to agree that hippies have some kind of widespread appeal, but nobody can say exactly what they stand for. Not even the hippies seem to know, although some can be very articulate when it comes to details.

"I love the whole world," said a 23-year-old girl in San Francisco's Haight-Ashbury district, the hippies' world capital. "I am the divine mother, part of Buddha, part of God, part of everything.

"I live from meal to meal. I have no money, no possessions. Money is beautiful only when it's flowing; when it piles up, it's a hang-up. We take care of each other. There's always something to buy beans and rice for the group, and someone always sees that I get 'grass' [marijuana] or 'acid' [LSD]. I was in a mental hospital once because I tried to conform and play the game. But now I'm free and happy."

She was then asked whether she used drugs often. "Fairly," she replied. "When I find myself becoming confused I drop out and take a dose of acid. It's a shortcut to reality; it throws you right into it. Everyone should take it, even children. Why shouldn't they be enlightened early, instead of waiting till they're old? Human beings need total freedom. That's where God is at. We need to shed hypocrisy, dishonesty, and phoniness and go back to the purity of our childhood values."

The next question was "Do you ever pray?" "Oh yes," she said. "I pray in the morning sun. It nourishes me with its energy so I can spread my love and beauty and nourish others. I never pray for anything; I don't need anything. Whatever turns me on is a sacrament: LSD, sex, my bells, my colors.... That's the holy communion, you dig?" That's about the most definitive comment anybody's ever going to get from a practicing hippie.

Unlike beatniks, many of whom were writing poems and novels with the idea of becoming second-wave Kerouac's or Allen Ginsberg's, the hippie opinion-makers have cultivated among their followers a strong distrust of the written word. Journalists are mocked, and writers are called "type freaks." Because of this stylized ignorance, few hippies are really articulate. They prefer to communicate by dancing, or touching, or extrasensory perception (ESP). They talk, among themselves, about "love waves" and "vibrations" ("vibes") that come from other people. That leaves a lot of room for subjective interpretation, and therein lies the key to the hippies' widespread appeal.

This is not to say that hippies are universally loved. From coast to coast, the forces of law and order have confronted the hippies with extreme distaste. Here are some representative comments from a Denver, Colo, police lieutenant. Denver, he said, was becoming a refuge for "long-haired, vagrant, antisocial, psychopathic, dangerous drug users, who refer to themselves as a 'hippie subculture a group which rebels against society and is bound together by the use and abuse of dangerous drugs and narcotics."

They range in age, he continued, from 13 to the early 20's, and they pay for their minimal needs by "mooching, begging, and borrowing from each other, their friends, parents, and complete strangers.... It is not uncommon to find as many as 20 hippies living together in one small apartment, in a communal fashion, with their garbage and trash piled halfway to the ceiling in some cases."

One of his co-workers, a Denver detective, explained that hippies are easy prey for arrests, since "it is easy to search and locate their drugs and marijuana because they don't have any furniture to speak of, except for mattresses lying on the floor. They don't believe in any form of productivity," he said, "and in addition to a distaste for work, money, and material wealth, hippies believe in free love, legalized use of marijuana, burning draft cards, mutual love and help, a peaceful planet, and love for love's sake. They object to war and believe that everything and everybody except the police are beautiful."

Many so-called hippies shout "love" as a cynical password and use it as a smokescreen to obscure their own greed, hypocrisy, or mental deformities. Many hippies sell drugs, and although the vast majority of such dealers sell only enough to cover their own living expenses, a few net upward of $20,000 a year. A kilogram (2.2 pounds) of marijuana, for instance, costs about $35 in Mexico. Once across the border, it sells (as a kilo) for anywhere from $150 to $200. Broken down into 34 ounces, it sells for $15 to $25 an ounce, or $510 to $850 a kilo. The price varies from city to city, campus to campus, and coast to coast. "Grass" is generally cheaper in California than it is in the East. The profit margin becomes mind-boggling regardless of the geography when a $35 Mexican kilogram is broken down into individual "joints," or marijuana cigarettes, which sell on urban street corners for about a dollar each.

The risk naturally increases with the profit potential. It's one thing to pay for a trip to Mexico by bringing back three kilos and selling two in a circle of friends: The only risk there is the possibility of being searched and seized at the border. But a man who gets arrested for selling hundreds of "joints" to high school students on a St. Louis street corner can expect the worst when his case comes to court.

The British historian Arnold Toynbee, at the age of 78, toured San Francisco's Haight-Ashbury district and wrote his impressions for the London Observer. "The leaders of the Establishment," he said, "will be making the mistake of their lives if they discount and ignore the revolt of the hippies and many of the hippies' non-hippie contemporaries on the grounds that these are either disgraceful wastrels or traitors or else just silly kids who are sowing their wild oats."

Toynbee never really endorsed the hippies; he explained his affinity in the longer focus of history. If the human race is to survive, he said, the ethical, moral, and social habits of the world must change: The emphasis must switch from nationalism to mankind. And Toynbee saw in the hippies a hopeful resurgence of the basic humanitarian values that were beginning to seem to him and other long-range thinkers like a tragically lost cause in the war-poisoned atmosphere of the 1960s. He was not quite sure what the hippies really stood for, but since they were against the same things he was against (war, violence, and dehumanized profiteering), he was naturally on their side, and vice versa.

There is a definite continuity between the beatniks of the 1950s and the hippies of the 1960s. Many hippies deny this, but as an active participant in both scenes, I'm sure it's true. I was living in Greenwich Village in New York City when the beatniks came to fame during 1957 and 1958. I moved to San Francisco in 1959 and then to the Big Sur coast for 1960 and 1961. Then after two years in South America and one in Colorado, I was back in San Francisco, living in the Haight-Ashbury district, during 1964, 1965, and 1966. None of these moves was intentional in terms of time or place; they just seemed to happen. When I moved into the Haight-Ashbury, for instance, I'd never even heard that name. But I'd just been evicted from another place on three days' notice, and the first cheap apartment I found was on Parnassus Street, a few blocks above Haight.

At that time the bars on what is now called "the street" were predominantly Negro. Nobody had ever heard the word "hippie," and all the live music was Charlie Parker-type jazz. Several miles away, down by the bay in the relatively posh and expensive Marina district, a new and completely unpublicized nightclub called the Matrix was featuring an equally unpublicized band called the Jefferson Airplane. At about the same time, hippie author Ken Kesey (One Flew Over the Cuckoo's Nest, 1962, and Sometimes a Great Notion, 1964) was conducting experiments in light, sound, and drugs at his home at La Honda, in the wooded hills about 50 miles south of San Francisco.

As the result of a network of circumstance, casual friendships, and connections in the drug underworld, Kesey's band of Merry Pranksters was soon playing host to the Jefferson Airplane and then to the Grateful Dead, another wildly electric band that would later become known on both coasts along with the Airplane as the original heroes of the San Francisco acid-rock sound. During 1965, Kesey's group staged several much-publicized Acid Tests, which featured music by the Grateful Dead and free Kool-Aid spiked with LSD. The same people showed up at the Matrix, the Acid Tests, and Kesey's home in La Honda. They wore strange, colorful clothes and lived in a world of wild lights and loud music. These were the original hippies.

It was also in 1965 that I began writing a book on the Hell's Angels, a notorious gang of motorcycle outlaws who had plagued California for years, and the same kind of weird coincidence that jelled the whole hippie phenomenon also made the Hell's Angels part of the scene. I was having a beer with Kesey one afternoon in a San Francisco tavern when I mentioned that I was on my way out to the headquarters of the Frisco Angels to drop off a Brazilian drum record that one of them wanted to borrow. Kesey said he might as well go along, and when he met the Angels he invited them down to a weekend party in La Honda. The Angels went and thereby met a lot of people who were living in the Haight-Ashbury for the same reason I was (cheap rent for good apartments).

People who lived two or three blocks from each other would never realize it until they met at some pre-hippie party. But suddenly everybody was living in Haight-Ashbury, and this accidental unity took on a style of its own. All that it lacked was a label, and the San Francisco Chronicle quickly came up with one. These people were "hippies," said the Chronicle, and, lo, the phenomenon was launched. The Airplane and the Grateful Dead began advertising their sparsely attended dances with psychedelic posters, which were given away at first and then sold for $1 each until finally, the poster advertisements became so popular that some of the originals were selling in the best San Francisco art galleries for more than $2,000. By this time both the Jefferson Airplane and the Grateful Dead had gold-plated record contracts, and one of the Airplane's best numbers, "White Rabbit," was among the best-selling singles in the nation.

By that time, too, the Haight-Ashbury had become such a noisy mecca for freaks, drug peddlers, and curiosity seekers that it was no longer a good place to live. Haight Street was so crowded that municipal buses had to be rerouted because of the traffic jams.

At the same time, the "Hashbury" was becoming a magnet for a whole generation of young dropouts, all those who had canceled their reservations on the great assembly line: the high-rolling, soul-bending competition for status and security in the ever-fattening yet ever-narrowing American economy of the late 1960s. As the rewards of status grew richer, the competition grew stiffer. A failing grade in math on a high school report card carried far more serious implications than simply a reduced allowance: It could alter a boy's chances of getting into college and, on the next level, of getting the "right job." As the economy demanded higher and higher skills, it produced more and more technological dropouts. The main difference between hippies and other dropouts was that most hippies were white and voluntarily poor. Their backgrounds were largely middle class; many had gone to college for a while before opting out for the "natural life." An easy, unpressured existence on the fringe of the money economy. Their parents, they said, were walking proof of the fallacy of the American notion that says "work and suffer now; live and relax later."

The hippies reversed that ethic. "Enjoy life now," they said, "and worry about the future tomorrow." Most take the question of survival for granted, but in 1967, as their enclaves in New York and San Francisco filled up with penniless pilgrims, it became obvious that there was simply not enough food and lodging.

A partial solution emerged in the form of a group called the Diggers, sometimes referred to as the "worker-priests" of the hippie movement. The Diggers are young and aggressively pragmatic; they set up free lodging centers, free soup kitchens, and free clothing distribution centers. They comb hippie neighborhoods, soliciting donations of everything from money to stale bread and camping equipment. in the Hashbury, Diggers' signs are posted in local stores, asking for donations of hammers, saws, shovels, shoes, and anything else that vagrant hippies might use to make themselves at least partially self-supporting. The Ashbury Diggers were able, for a while, to serve free meals, however meager, each afternoon in Golden Gate Park, but the demand soon swamped the supply. More and more hungry hippies showed up to eat, and the Diggers were forced to roam far afield to get food.

The concept of mass sharing goes along with the American-Indian tribal motif that is basic to the whole hippie movement. The cult of tribalism is regarded by many as the key to survival. Poet Gary Snyder, one of the hippie gurus, or spiritual guides, sees a "back to the land" movement as the answer to the food and lodging problem. He urges hippies to move out of the cities, form tribes, purchase land, and live communally in remote areas. By early 1967 there were already a half dozen functioning hippie settlements in California, Nevada, Colorado, and upstate New York. They were primitive shack-towns, with communal kitchens, half-alive fruit and vegetable gardens, and spectacularly uncertain futures.

Back in the cities, the vast majority of hippies were still living from day to day. On Haight Street, those without gainful employment could easily pick up a few dollars a day by panhandling. The influx of nervous voyeurs and curiosity seekers was a handy money tree for the legion of psychedelic beggars. Regular visitors to the Hashbury found it convenient to keep a supply of quarters in their pockets so that they wouldn't have to haggle about change. The panhandlers were usually barefoot, always young, and never apologetic. They would share what they collected anyway, so it seemed entirely reasonable that strangers should share with them. Unlike the beatniks, few hippies are given to strong drink. Booze is superfluous in the drug culture, and food is regarded as a necessity to be acquired at the least possible expense. A "family" of hippies will work for hours over an exotic stew or curry, but the idea of paying three dollars for a meal in a restaurant is out of the question.

Some hippies work, others live on money from home, and many get by with part-time jobs, loans from old friends, or occasional transactions on the drug market. In San Francisco, the post office is a major source of hippie income. Jobs like sorting mail don't require much thought or effort. The sole support of one "clan" (or "family," or "tribe") was a middle-aged hippie known as Admiral Love, of the Psychedelic Rangers, who had a regular job delivering special delivery letters at night. There was also a hippie-run employment agency on Haight Street; anyone needing temporary labor or some kind of specialized work could call up and order whatever suitable talents were available at the moment.

Significantly, the hippies have attracted more serious criticism from their former compatriots of the New Left than they have from what would seem to be their natural antagonists on the political right. Conservative William Buckley's National Review, for instance, says, "The hippies are trying to forget about original sin and it may go hard with them hereafter." The National Review editors completely miss the point that serious hippies have already dismissed the concept of original sin and that the idea of a hereafter strikes them as a foolish, anachronistic joke. The concept of some vengeful God sitting in judgment on sinners is foreign to the whole hippie ethic. Its God is a gentle abstract deity not concerned with sin or forgiveness but manifesting himself in the purest instincts of "his children."

The New Left brand of criticism has nothing to do with theology. Until 1964, in fact, the hippies were so much a part of the New Left that nobody knew the difference. "New Left," like "hippie" and "beatnik," was a term coined by journalists and headline writers, who need quick definitions of any subject they deal with. The term came out of the student rebellion at the University of California's Berkeley campus in 1964 and 1965. What began as a Free Speech Movement in Berkeley soon spread to other campuses in the East and Midwest and was seen in the

Chapter 1. Life At Home

Aileen & her brother Keith.

Earliest Memories

My memory of my kid days can go way back. So far back I amaze myself! Such as, I can recall being held in a boy's blanket with 3 women standing around staring at me and playing with my hands and nose, all of which I didn't like at all haha.

Then I remember another scene being real little. I was in a crib where my diapers were on too tight and the safety pins were digging into my hips, with me wanting this taken care of royal. As I cried my heart out for them to come and rescue me.

And as I moved on into the growing pains of life, I'd come across a hot interest that'd intrigue me so. All of which would be music. I fell in love! Dazzled in Rock and Roll. I was gonna be another Janis Joplin or Jimmy Hendrix. You name it...

Then I started getting musical equipment for Christmas. I was gearing up for a band! I had acquired now Bongo's, a flute, and a harmonica. But best of all... a windup guitar! Yet low and behold, I could never master those frigging strings and the fancy art of playing it. So I'd wind it up instead, allowing it to strum itself. "This land is your land" as I'd pretend I was Hendrix haha.

The Neighborhood Where Aileen Grew Up

The house we lived in was built by my dad, cousins, and friends. While mom prettied it up with flower gardens...

Well ol' lost buddy. Send more pictures of you, of everyone if you can. If you could someday soon. Would you please take a couple color photos of my old house? It sits across from the Maddox's. Please do. I'd like to see if my Mothers flowers are still around. And her trees she raised...

***

From the looks of my old house in this photo, I stand in Awe! Totally amazed! The front door – "look at it closely!" it seems to be like some 20/30 inches from the screen door. Which has me believe they re-converted the Living room.

The tree in the front yard is new. Some 23 years old, but wasn't my mom's doing. She planted 2 trees in the back, close to the house and I see they're still there. Barry engraved his name at the top of the tree, one facing west – from the back yard – (left hand one.) So if anyone ever cuts it down, they'll see his name and date on the bark.

The flowers are all gone! My mom worked for 33 years on all her flower beds. And the rose bushes that use to line the house and the aluminum chain fencing that is now gone used to be around the front yard.

The middle section of the house we called the backroom. I feel was remodeled inside... They either built another fireplace or this new gray smoke stack deal above the house is for the sauna in the garage which maybe they kept and didn't tear down. The sauna was a steam room, 'Finnish style', my Dad built it along with the house...

Say did you notice if the names on the mailboxes were still our ol' kid friends? Like their parents still live there, or kids took over after perhaps their deaths. Like Kerr's or Maddox's or Farewells.

I'm very happy to see my house has been so cared for and as creatively kept up with as it has been. Whoever lives there thank you!

***

Hellooo! And Thank you for the greatest gift you could've ever given this gal locked up... I love ya Buddy! Last night I went to the 70s and just was flooded with the good old days... I'm curious if the woods next to my house are still there. So are there woods there? These woods we would gallivant through to reach the pits.

I remember saving Lori's butt from some bees in those woods next to Randall's.

Me probably 9 or 10, her 11 or 12. There was this abandoned car, Chevy-looking, we were goofing around by it. We lifted the wood near the vehicle and out came the bees, swarming everywhere, we ran, yet they kept coming.

She was stung about 5 times only! Should have been more. Did I get any thanks for it? Haha, hell no! Only; "It was your fault, your fault, your fault." Chuckle, chuckle.

Always trying to be a hero to my sis. Carl Maddox had this bow and arrow set. Always was over our house trying to shoot bats with it. I watched the arrow coming down zeroing on Lori. The arrow hit her in the back. It wasn't in far. About a 1/2 inch or less but still had to be removed. So I removed it... she didn't want mom + Dad to know. So I put peroxide and iodine on it, stuck a band-aide across it. And Wallah Some 4 days later she was OK. Was I credited? Heck no! not this time either. It was you and Carl's fault, you and Carl's, you and Carl's. Haha, boy oh boy! Memories!

I really am grateful for these flicks. I wish I could see the back trees in the backyard. Those 2 my mom planted when the house was built. Lots of tree climbing we did in those babies. Love ya Forever! Aileen

***

These pictures are the greatest! I need to thank you over and over again! See the little window up in the attic area of the house, above to the left, over on the roof area of the backroom. Well, that little window is where Keith, Lori, and I use to skip out. This was so we could head out to the pits – when parties were going on.

As for Randall's house, well, I bet Lori wished their house was like this one instead of what the Randall's did exist as. Their house was a shamble with all the kids. All boys at that.! I never could understand how Lori could live with them. Although I guess it was tolerable because Keith also lived with them.

Me I was able to too... in the abandoned car on the cinder blocks in the yard. Remember hahaha?! There was no room anywhere in the house to sleep, so the car was the only option. I think I slept there for about 3 months or more.

Once winter came, I couldn't take it anymore, so I headed to Florida...

Nick Broomfield Driving Round The Neighborhood

Nick voice-over: Michelle drove us to Aileen's old home, they grew up as Vietnam was ending, and drugs were everywhere.

Michelle: Aileen's house was right over there, you want to go by it?

Joan: Yeah!

Michelle: OK, I'll take you by it, this was Mark Faron's house, we were all connected together, we all used to hang in the neighborhood you know, all the kids packed together. This was Terry Cox's house, she used to do a lot of drugs with XXXX. This is Aileen's house right here, this is it, this was her house.

Nick: And when you saw her being beaten...

Michelle: Erm yeah that door right there, I was in front of that door, see they've redone the house since then, but that room in the very back is her bedroom, not the first one but the second window, you see how low they are, she used to climb right out of them. XXXX lived there also and we used to go over and smoke pot and do whatever, get in all kinds of shit.

Nick: But lot's of different drugs?

Michelle: Yes! Erm lots of pills actually, LSD, mescaline, bladder acid.

The 1ˢᵗ Picture is of Aileen (center) with her brother Keith (right), and sister and brother Barry & Lori (biological uncle and auntie). The 2ⁿᵈ picture is of Aileen's parents (biological grandparents) with her biological mom Diane.

Rebel Kid

The Night Before Christmas

And talk about good-looking, my parents reminded me of Movie Stars royal! They tried their best to keep the morals in the family and in tune to it too. So it wasn't really all that bad. As things wouldn't change until we'd reach our teens. Lord there went our moral values, be it the booze, cigs, or drugs.

You know sitting here thinking of Christmas got me remembering when Keith and I were little young's and a real cute incident occurred Haha. Let me share it with ya, OK? We were no other than me 6, Keith 7, Lori 8 and Barry 10. A perfect Christmas Eve.

After hours of fun, and time for bed, we hit it worn out yet not willing to sleep, so we could hopefully catch Santa. So we stayed up.

45 minutes had to of gone by, when suddenly Keith, shrieked. "I see him!" "I see him!" "I just saw a red cap go by the front door, He's here!" And scurried he did – to the fireplace – to cordially Welcome Santa down the shoot. While Lori and I ran to the front door.

All the commotion gave us away, as mom and Dad stumbled on into the living room to witness us all up and about! Scolded, we were hurried back to bed. Well so be it, mom and Dad knew when all of us were asleep. Cause none of us with them placing all the gifts that night, we so faithfully requested to Santa. Every year our ways of doing it up for the Holidays were pretty much likewise. Our imaginations were running wild and free – full of exciting fun. Until we had to learn the truth. Final outcome, Keith got bombarded with snowballs the rest of the winter hahaha.

Childhood Smoking

Strawberries, yum, sounds good. Haven't had lovely strawberries since I was 6 or 7. So it's been a long time. And when we were kids we tried to smoke the rotted vines. It worked a little. You could get a puff or 2. But we started early with cigarettes, so continued to rip em off from whomever or wherever we could. As for having put out for any, no way. And whoever made that one up is CRAZY, period. Anyway, kid days! Ahhhh, they were so heavenly.

Playing With Fire

School became my favorite thing to attend. But when 3rd grade would come along, this would take a turn for the worse, screwing up my joy of going.

I was 9 and Lori was 11 at the time and I decided to play with some flammable liquid in an empty duck shed we had alongside our house. The whole shed lit up quick, being so full of hay and rotted wood. As Lori received a slight burn on her thigh, and me, my face.

1st and 2nd-degree burns they were. Some 3rd around the forehead. Luckily it was basically lighter fluid and not gasoline or I'd of been without one, a face that is, for sure.

I was wrapped up like the invisible man for at least 3 days in the Hospital. Then for a time at home. After about 3 months it seemed, caring for the burns, I'd wind up with scars on my forehead only, thank God! And I always have.

Yet this didn't heed any warning signals to be more careful... I began to also become one hell of a runaway. Skipping out the house at least every 3 months once the age of 13 would arrive.

So my rebellious butt kept saying, "freedom!" As off I'd go. As further troubles came my way. Only to cause then one word to be so hated by me so much so that it would be enough to kill.

Chapter 2. Runaway Kid

Aileen aged 13. A happy moment during one of her family's regular summer vacations & Aileen riding her bike in her Troy neighborhood.

First Rapes (Aged 13)

My first run-in with rape would be at parties I was considered a stranger to. Out in Pontiac and Detroit. Whereas I'd find myself tied to a bed spread eagle, that is once I awoke and gang-raped. As I'd run into at least 3 of these brutal attacks at 13. Animals.

Then sadly I was running into this with those I knew at parties. And then the last to come which hindered anymore for a while anyway would be from a ride, as I'd hitchhike home from Clawson after sneaking out to party at, some 8 miles away. And this one would get me pregnant. At 14. Low Life Scum Ball.

The guy said he knew my dad, and where I lived. He picked me up out of the pouring rain on 20 and Rochester, across from the Clark station. He pulled me out of it and asked me if I could use a lift. I told him where I lived, not far! Then he said my dad's name, he said he comes to the bar often. Then the rest.. too embarrassing.

Then trying to hide it for six months which was only getting harder to do. Talk about then adding insult to injury! I was sent to an unwed home in Detroit. Only to then have to put him up for adoption once born.

Abusers & The Negligent

This notion of yours that if only you'd a done more as a kid for me! Quit! There was no way you could help. You were a teen, you had no way to! Your parents couldn't either, being as barely making it themselves + for you 3. Others could have helped me in life but didn't. Instead, abused me or tried to in one way or the other. These ones are definitely to blame. So pleeeeeease don't ever feel guilty about such. No need to, OK? God knows precisely who they are.

Unwed Mothers Home In Detroit (Aged 14)

It's snowing outside. Way back when I was 14, stuck in an unwed mothers home in Detroit, low and behold just before I had the little tike it was snowing outside. Boy, that kid I had was huge. I can't remember if they said 7 lbs 11 ounces or 11 lbs 7 ounces. But I sure remember well the pain. 24 hours of labor. The stretch marks from him rack my body. They're all over. He pulled me apart!

I wound up naming him Keith Arnold Wuornos. Then later, as I was being sentenced to girls training school. the Judge said that my child was adopted into a wealthy family and that the 1st name was kept. Hmm. Wonder how true that all was. Anyway, it sure kept me happy!

Mother's Death (Biological Grandmother)

My dad got laid off of Beaver Precision after 15 years there...

I believe this is where the major problems in the house began. Him there 24/7 drunk.

That's when Dad began to hit the bottle more than ever before and my Mother unknowingly was getting sicker of a sickness I didn't know she even had.

Mom would die from the thyroid condition and Dad would later commit suicide over it.

My mother wound up dying in one of the bedrooms of the house, as dad Would later bet the house away with a horse bet at Hazel Park Race Track. Then later I'd learn that he assisted Mom to her death. By getting what she requested for the first time ever, since she didn't drink at all. And that was beer to increase her chances and as the story goes to ease the pains of, from this thyroid condition that gave her this sclerosis of the Liver.

I was crushed. Had I only known, I know I would have tried to "then" straighten things out between Dad and me. I became crushed to the max. I hitchhiked to her funeral and then a short time later would be picked up for the first time as a runaway.

***

I've got to tell you something that'll blow your mind like it has mine. I mean this is awesome.! When I was a kid my mom + I would talk about God and life after death, and besides hundreds of other things – also the house being fixed up. She died then when I was 14.

Well, I was around 9 or 10 when Dad finally decided to get aluminum siding for the house. Mom was in big hopes to also get shutters for all the Windows. White ones at that! But Dad could only afford the siding and that's all. she kept her hopes up high for someday – getting those shutters for the house. Well, she died before this could ever be fulfilled. Yet! LOOK! Today there are white shutters. As if the people who moved in were influenced by my mom's spirit...

Well, there's more!

My mom was getting interested in planting more trees. She had 2 planted in the back... But here in the early 70s, she wanted to plant more.

So, these people who now live here, have done precisely again – another gig – exactly as my mom had planned but never fulfilled. Woe! Awesome ay?!

I say it's a sign from my mom. Because when we were little and talks on God would come up. she often mentioned that if she was to die, she'd love to be able to leave "Signs" somehow that / regardless out of the body / she's still alive. She even thought of one idea, that. was to clip a rose off of one of her many rose bushes., place it in a vase without water on the fireplace mantel. If the rose didn't wilt in a week but stayed fresh as if just clipped off the bush, it was done by her, as proof, she is still alive "in Spirit". Well, Lori and Dad did do this, and the rose stayed good for not only a week. But a week and a 1/2. At least this is what Lori told me. Awesome Ay?!

Father's Abuse (Biological Grandfather)

'I Hated Him'

From my experiences with my father. I hated him! On a lot of occasions of how he seemingly institutionalized me at home. He was as cold as ice. All because of WWII. He was a sergeant in it, head over 50 men while fighting in his platoon. And he felt like Keith + I were the enemy. had invaded his territory. So like a syndrome. he laid his "Sergeant crap" on us. Even having us forced to call him "Sir". instead of dad.

2nd Class Children

Hey, remember when I was trying to explain why I think Lori and Barry were different from Keith and me genetically. OK, what I was trying to say was that Diane was their 1st child. So my grandparents' gene's probably weren't as destroyed yet from booze. Like my grandfathers. So Diane's makeup was OK, but Barry and Lori came next afterward, and I believe now dads sperm count wasn't so good as when Diane was brought forth into the world. So with it off in genetics, not much, but enough to warrant a slight characteristics problem, once they were birthed. Lori + Barry both Graduated + Barry went to college. See Keith and I's neglection by the family, in being always 2nd class, had us "run away from home."

If mom hadn't died. I bet Lori could've gone to college also. But had we wanted to? No go! So now you see why Lori & Barry would jump on the money to witness against me. Lying for the state and for the money.

Time for me to study my Bible, Stay Cool.

The Kiddo! Love Aileen.

A Memory Of One Of Her Dad's Savage Beatings

Michelle: I don't know how much you want me to say, he was a bastard.

Lawyer: Do you recall an incident when you and Aileen skipped school.

Michelle: Yes.

Lawyer: What happened? Did you go up to Aileen's house?

Michelle: I walked home with her, and we had gotten caught, and I remember looking through the front, they had a screen door view, and the minute she walked in, he had her over a chair, and ah *sighs* I stood there and watched him, and he beat the hell out of her with a black belt that was around his waist, he took it off and told her to lean over the chair, and he walloped on her for a good 5 minutes.

Lawyer: Is this what you would call a spanking?

Michelle: Oh no, no, it was like, it left me hypnotized.

Lawyer: Did he know you were watching?

Michelle: Yea he did, he was aware I was watching.

Lawyer: Is that just an example as to...

Michelle: That's an example, yes.

Nick Broomfield Interview

Nick voice-over: I wondered how Aileen herself viewed her childhood in Troy.

Nick: Was it quite nice living there?

Aileen: Yeah Troy's alright, and oh... I want to straighten out something man, say hey Nick, I want to get this straightened out because Jacky, Drew and all of them, all lied about my family.

Nick: Well how did they lie about your family?

Aileen: Well see, now I gotta, this documentation, I've got to square some stuff up.

Nick: OK so tell me about your family.

Aileen: OK the truth about my family is this, my dad was so straight and so clean, he wouldn't even wear a, take his shirt off to mow the lawn. He did not believe in cussing, he did not believe in er long hair and miniskirts and stuff, he was really straight and real decent. And so was my mom, my mom hated swearing in the house, if you swore, you said one swear word, you'd have a whole bar of lava soap in your mouth, so I came from a real clean and decent family.

Nick: But why then did you get thrown out after the birth?

Aileen: See after my mom died, my dad got pissed; he was like "OK this is the last straw," you know, "I think you are the cause of mom's death." Because she had physical problems because of all the stress and the pain of everything, you know? And what I'm going through as a wild kid is pissing him off. I mean he thinks that that killed her as well, and induced her death, so he's pissed off, he doesn't want me home anymore.

Nick: Aileen, let me ask you one question, do you think if you hadn't had to leave your home and sleep in the cars and stuff, your life would have turned out differently?

Aileen: Now then [back to serious], if I could do my life all over again and I came from backgrounds that were right on [betrays script], I mean my family was right on, but as far as my mom not dying, my dad not freaking out about us. If I could do it all over again, my family died too young, I had to hit the road, and I came from a supportive family, we didn't have split sister and brother stuff and all that, it was all true blood, all of that blood and everything was, financially stable, and everybody was really tight... I [pauses for effect], would have become more than likely an outstanding citizen of America, who would have either been an archaeologist, a paramedic, a police officer, a fire department gal, or an undercover worker for DEA, or did I say archaeology? Or a missionary, but I'm not a Christian freak, so scrub missionary, because I'm just thinking you know, if I would have come from a decent, ye know I would have done real decent.

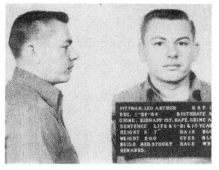

The young Diane Wuornos, Aileen and Keith's natural mother who abandoned her when she was 4 years old.

& Leo Pittman, Aileen's natural father, eventually committed suicide in prison. Sentenced to life behind bars for raping a seven-year-old.

Biological Mother

Interview With Aileen's Biological Mother

Nick voice-over: We're driving to meet Dianne Wuornos, Aileen's Biological mother, they haven't laid eyes on each other for 25 years, this is Calumet, a copper mining town on Michigan's upper peninsular, the Wuornos family originally came here as immigrants from, Owlo in Finland to work down the mines.

Dianne: OK, I want to tell you something about her birth, she was a frank breech birth, that means bottom first, and a breech birth is very dangerous, and that's feet first, and a frank breach, is really very bad, the doctor even called in other people to watch it, because it was so unusual but I thought maybe she got some kind of brain damage during that birth, because it was so unusual, and that while she's mentally competent, it may have caused her problems. What does Aileen think about what caused her to act like that?

Nick: Well originally she said she did it in self-defense, then she said she just needed the money. She says that if she came from a home that wasn't split...

Dianne: Oh because of her father and me getting a divorce.

Nick: She didn't say that. I think she's confused because on the one hand says it had nothing to do with her childhood, but then on the other hand she was sleeping out in the snow for a while and living in the woods.

Dianne: She was sleeping in the snow and living in the woods?

Nick: Immediately after she had the baby.

Dianne: I know nothing about that? I never heard Barry tell me that.

Nick: After she had the baby she couldn't move back into the house with your father, then she was living in the woods in the snow.

Dianne: Didn't agency find her and take care of her?

Nick: No, and then she ended up hitching around.

Dianne: Which she liked.

(long pause)

Dianne: Do you know the exact date of the execution?

Nick: I think it's soon.

Dianne: OK, I think I'll rest better.

Nick voice-over: As we were leaving, Dianne asked for Aileen's forgiveness.

Nick Broomfield Interview

Nick: Just before we came here, we met with your mother Dianne

Aileen: You met with my brother and Dianne, I could give a...

Nick: Your mother Dianne

Aileen: My mother Dianne, let me tell you something about my mother, she plopped me out of her belly, left me with my grandparents, and we never knew her, so tell that damn whore, I could give a fuck if she even had me, she had me and left, to Texas, my mom and my dad never saw them ever again, except at funerals, my moms funeral, my dads funeral, and my brothers funeral. And if she's at mine, probably be spitting on her, I couldn't care less; I don't give a damn about that damn whore. I don't know her, I never even knew her.

Nick: Well she asked for your forgiveness

Aileen: She can go to hell, she doesn't have any of my forgiveness, I don't even know her, don't even want to know her.

Chapter 3. Institutionalization

Pontiac Juvenile center (Aged 15)

Well, as you know, way back, at the age of 15, I ran away from home for the 3rd and last time. The other times were at the age of 13 and 14. Now Mom cared, but Dad didn't. But, for themselves not to get in any trouble with the Law, they did as any normal parent should do and finally filed a runaway report. With Dad having a plan behind it once I was caught, which I had no idea of.

Then of course, as you know, during this 3rd split from the house, Mom dies. Unaware to! I had no idea she was so sick. As she died in the morning, and I was at the pits about to be hunted down by Lori and some of the Shelley girls in Dad's Maverick that Lori was driving.

Now you may have been with them Dawn, but I can't remember everyone there. I was beginning to get way burned out from the whole mess, so please forgive me if you were and I've forgotten. Anyway, from the car someone came down to the beach and told me Lori was up there and needed to talk with me. So, I made my way up the embankment to the car, only to find her full of tears. Then she laid on the shocking news and split, just to leave me likewise.

The news got to the cops fast, that I was around the area after that. Surely by Lori, Barry or Dad. But because of an uncle or cousin, I can't remember what kind of king he was, being one of the Cops in Troy I believe I was overlooked for a while as a runaway, so I could attend her funeral.

Yet it wouldn't be 24 hours later after I did that I'd sure enough be rounded up on my way to a juvenile facility out in Pontiac.

Now let me tell ya, that center was something else. Full of yuck and disgust. Hate was everywhere! And nothing was being accomplished because of it.

And it wouldn't be 2 days there, that I'd get locked down in a tiny cell away from the others for giving a Matron the finger. I believe they left me in there around a week or so, as the one I gave the finger to, knew very well about my Mom's death. Having just died. But did they care?! Why hell no! Only that the information was music to their ears to further punish me with. So they Loved it, and snickered anytime I mentioned here name or memories of.

Then one day came a break. A good way to bust from the place. The girls were heading on a field trip and I was asked to come along. I figured, excellent, now I can run from this joint. As my feet began to itch with excitement. I had a trail to blaze.

Finally, by another week we were off. Arriving at a picnic area that was way out in the Boonies. I kept looking around and saying to myself... How easy! And once everyone was pretty well occupied. I walked off. I must've been a good ½ mile when they finally noticed me missing! And then way in the distance, I could hear them calling my name. As I just laughed and walked on.

Around 2 miles or more I found a farm. My eyes trained on the barn as a hideout, I started towards it only to be greeted by 2 young guys and an older man who was part of the farm. The father and sons. They immediately started asking me what I was doing on their land. As I really didn't much care and told them everything. They told me they heard plenty about the place and its cruel conditions so decided to help me.

They hid me then up in the Barn until the coast was clear – as meanwhile, their Mom was making sandwiches and soup for us all. After it'd get dark they were then gonna take me to I-75, and with great thanks, I'd be back on my way to Troy – hitchhiking.

3 Weeks On The Run, Partying, Then Back In Court

As to say the 1st day on the run, it went swell. While for 3 more weeks I'd be back around everybody to see and party with. Only to then get busted again and wind up back at the facility.

The court appearances didn't take long. I didn't have one the first go around. They just called my Dad up and he said he didn't want me anymore. But this time one was up, as I was appearing on charges of Run Away. And there was Dad, alone and smelling as usual full of wine. He kept giving me a dirty eye and telling me he couldn't wait for this to be over with and to never have to see me again. As if I was going to be hanged.

But I guess it wasn't gonna work for ol' Dad the way he wanted it. When the judge asked if he wanted me back home, he shouted from the rooftop "no!" And to "do as you like to her, but she'll never step foot in my house again!" So the judge sentenced me to 6 months in Adrian, to a place known as a girls training school. Leaving me and my Dad with these words before pounding the gavel, "Maybe by then you'll change your mind about her, And me about running away from home."

I'd stare Dad dead in the eyes and tell the man I hated his guts. As he'd stare back and tell me he never wanted to see me again. And it'd be nearly the last too! With the exception of a few more run in's now and then before he commits suicide over everything! Especially the loss of his beloved wife.

Then the place I was sent to. Man. Was it a trip...

Adrian's Girls School

Let me tell ya some of the ol' wars I've been in hahaha. I've got scads of war stories! Seen a bunch! Chuckle Chuckle. So as I said I'd do. Let me continue here with Adrian. Lord. Now that, there, is one war story! Geeeez.

Arriving in the evening hours to check into my new motel or should I say hell, called Girls Training School. Located in Adrian Michigan.

I was amazed at how huge the place was! It was once an old plantation... As the houses with all their buildings intrigued me with their antiquity.

I pictured Amish folk or even further than that! The 1500 pilgrims or others. Visualizing them wandering around. To be now remodeled into a reformatory for troubled Kids and run away's like me.

I was placed in a cottage named Rose, I believe! Two more weeks of thee ol' place and I was suddenly getting homesick... and wanting to just get back to Troy to see Keith and Lori again. Or anybody else I loved! So plans of running were next... The place was so wide open you could just walk away. So I figured. A piece of cake!

Oh, but I'd learn a tail of major problems. As the story went, that no girl had yet succeeded in her attempts. Because of the hounds.

What?! There it was. Well, OK, back to the drawing board, and how I'm gonna beat them hounds once I take off.

The 1st Run

Hi Buddy! Ready for some more Adrian. I hope so, cause here comes a bunch more. Enjoy the campfire talk. Chuckle. Chuckle. Hand me another marshmallow will ya. One of those dam hounds took the last one I had on the stick. Hahaha boy them hounds! So it went like this Dawn.

A Black gal named Bernadette and I volunteered Kitchen duty After Breakfast, we had to wait for roll call and one more round of a check from the cottage guard when Bernadette gave me the signal to hit it, and I was gone!

Suddenly... the dog looked up from sniffing and stared right at me. He just stopped at all that he was doing and stared right in my direction. Then the farmer said: "you see something boy?!". as he began to look in my direction too. I nearly fell out! My heart was in my throat! I kept eyeing them and thinking... I'm busted. But not without a fight! when next the dog went back to snooping the tracks and moving on, as the farmer took the dog's word for it, and followed on behind him.

I started laughing. Here they both passed me up, right from under their noses.

Boooom! Out the back door I flew! Running my ass off! Crossing the dirt road, flying over the ditch into the woods, just running as fast as I could. I was flooring it right through the pine, brush, and shrub, slipping along the way on broken limbs and pine cones laying around!

This running was Hard. My legs were growing tired, as my chest was wretched in Sweat and Pain. Burning Bad! This burning ripped down my throat and licked flat into my lungs like fire.

I knew I had to keep running and get a good mile or two before I could stop, but feeling ½ way there is when I heard the hounds.

So the more I heard those hounds, the faster I ran. My body felt like it was gonna just drop...

I knew then too, that I had to hide out near the tracks and just hope for the better.

And as the hounds were getting closer and closer – I feared only 2 things bad! The pounding of my heart. and sweat. Wondering if the dogs would pick up any of it.

Eyeing the ties, I began to see what was hunting me down. it was one huge fat guy with farmer jeans and a flannel shirt on. With one dog! They were so close, I could hear the dogs panting.

Don't get scared now. Cause later on there's even scarier hahaha. I swear. Enjoy my stories, buddy. What a life I lead. For sure.

So in continuance here. I must have gotten 100 yards when suddenly out of the blue came another guy with a dog. But this time in the woods. The girls told me to wear dark colors if I was gonna do this, so I put on a black T-shirt with blue jeans. It obviously did the trick too! Because in this 2nd run-in they just walked on by saying to myself Man! your Dogs can't smell. Unless the dog was just caught up in the matrix of the woods. / with its smell and all. Therefore blocking his scent. Otherwise, these dogs were just phony to me! as they walked on by...

I now wondered how many more of them there were.

I trucked it back up on the tracks and started running. I was amazed! Not a soul in sight! But, I could see a problem ahead. The woods were diminishing into a cow pasture and lots of it! Now all you could see was green grass! Acres of it! All looking like a huge golf course in every direction for miles!

So my next plan was to get off. But where?! There was nothing.

Nothing but a Huge Tree that really branched out itself I figured I'd park my butt under it and pray for the best while I rested up some too. God knows my lungs were burning. So were the muscles of my legs I was completely drained and exhausted.

When I finally did reach the tree I noticed a small community of houses down in the Valley. As another wonder crossed my mind if I could be easily spotted under it? Once again I just prayed for the best I just panted away – leaning against [the tree].

I sat under that tree just talking away to God. And how I missed my Mom so bad. that No One would ever take her place.

Then I began to do some sinful praying. Asking him to help me get through the run. And once I could reach the outskirts and highway, to help me hitchhike it back to Troy.

And then suddenly. It seemed like out of nowhere. came this guy. He said "You know it was a long walk to get to ya you mind if I sit against the tree here with ya and catch my breath?!" I said. "I don't care!" So he sat down then he said real sympathetic like "You're from that Girls training School aren't ya?!"

The hair of my head started risen with my adrenaline as well. I must have looked like a scared horse, when I said, "No." He said. "Yes you are, Cause you see here I've got a picture of ya!" And he handed me the picture. I glared at the Juvenile Mug shot and thought to throw it and run. But he must have sensed it, cause he suddenly grabbed me by the wrist and held on tight saying; "Don't try it, see those cars down there, they're full of hounds!" Best give up cause you're surrounded. They've got ya hon." Looking around, and realizing he was right I gave up all my hard efforts and surrendered.

We slowly walked over to around 4 carloads of dogs and people, as I was then placed in one and back on my way to Adrian.

Thinking. how much I struggled to get away and how fruitless it all became I then had to ask and said. Hey! By the way! How far are we from the School?! He Said 3 miles.

2nd Run

I was positioned at the door, readying myself for this fly-by-night run...

As my heart jumped in my mouth and my Adrenalin rushed to my head. I went for it! Yanking the door open having it smack against the wall.

Then, The chase was on!

Flooring it to the exit, With the girls out in the hall cheering me on, as I could hear them saying Go Go Go Go Go. Runnnnnnnnnnn!

I kept flying on down the stairs and could hear each step snapping under the Weight having me trembling to the ground.

I was bolting across the road, on into the dense forest debris, stumbling over this and tripping over that.

I couldn't see a thing! As a sense of direction seemed easy to be impaired. I wasn't liking this at all!

But, hey, I couldn't turn back now, it was Troy or die. My senses were desperate, as I went on to tough it out.

Butttt! I'd find out pushing through the woods in the middle of the night was like being lost in a cave without a flashlight. It was just too thick!

I'd suddenly run into a barbed wire fence the pillowcase blocked the blow. And started back at full speed...

So I started pushing harder, running as if the wind was at my back. With my heart pounding wild and lungs burning bad all over aching.

Just as soon as I thought I was clear of the fence a spool of barbed wire lying on the ground, swirled round and round, would greet me. Eat a pita. I was pissed!

Flying through the woods only to fall full force with one horrific impact, I did, onto this roll of spikes. Gouged from head to toe. given them hounds just what they needed to pick up a good scent.

I was pissed. Bad. Haha.

Back on my feet, flying through the woods. Not knowing how much damage had been done, being chased by a pack of hounds and running like a wild animal.

But I wasn't giving up! No way! I was too desperate for Troy. As I struggled on in a mess of blood, sweat, and tears.

Sometimes I was in a clearance of forestry getting a good run. Then to only reach brush and shrub, trudging through it with extreme difficulty. While my cuts just stung. It was a terrible aching mess when... Boom! I fell on another coiled-up spool of razor wire. Cussing up a storm!

As I pushed myself off and could relate to the feeling of the suffering of the cuts, bruises, and impalement's Jesus bore by the hands of such earthly forces. I couldn't believe it!

I was just a runaway. This was my crime. "Runaway".

I was pissed. It was insane. And then trapping the woods to catch an adolescent. Like this! I thought, are you crazy folks or what?! Geeeez!

And the damage being extensive just to help their hounds catch their prey. To do then what?!

Abuse the hell out of once it's caught. Well, they weren't going to get me!

It became useless, to hope the pain would end, the throbs tore through me.

But I was strung out to get away from that school and back home. As my home was Troy itself. So I kept hauling ass through everything!

When Low and Behold another swirl I'd smack into! Again! God was I mad. Woooooo!

This time landing spread eagle. Arms extended. Legs extended. Pillowcase went flying. And there I was.

Boy was I ever in pain!

I pushed myself off, as cloth sounds ripped through the cool of the midnight air. As I could hear the hounds gaining.

I immediately changed course, I went straight for the highway.

The start of my plan's from the get-go. To clear 3 miles of wood then hit the highway...

I figured the most I gained was ½ mile or so. As I kept cutting through the woods in my cut-up mess, searching blindly for the highway like a bat outta hell and a scared rabbit, as well.

Searching for signs of any highway nearby, I could hear the distant sounds of traffic and smell their fumes, so knew I was getting near.

But there was this one huge gouge – gored along my right Wrist (inside)... that left me in fear of bleeding to death...

Only to then frantically pull off my T-shirt, rip a piece off, and hopefully put a good tourniquet on it to stop the flow.

I hit pay dirt. There it was! Without a car in sight. And while I stood upon the road, from the light of the moon, for the first time could see the damage done over my clothes, shoes, everything! I could hear the hounds off in the distance.

Thinking No way am I heading back in those woods. But I did see a good size tree full of leaves and limbs and started up it.

So I sat up in that tree waiting for them trying hard to hide the pillowcase full of blood drops and smears of, with my arms crossed over it, and with legs drawn up, hoping to cover its view...

I could hear their voices now, as well as the dogs panting there were, 2 guys with 2 dogs...

The dogs picked up my scent and raced to the tree, barking up it. Viciously! I freaked! Oh My God!

Figuring surely I was busted.

Locked eye to eye, there we were, staring at each other, saying nothing...

Then the other guy asked if I was up there, as he kept shining his small flashlight at me only to then pull it away from me to other parts of the tree and say "no, I think the hounds are barking at a raccoon or a squirrel or something. But I don't see her."

I was awestruck! Totally wiped out. What I said to myself?! What the hell?!

I stayed up in that tree too, just encase there was anymore on their way. But there were none. As the fat fellas with their dogs were back not 20 minutes later it seemed they passed right on by heading back towards the school, with just one quick glance up by the one who let me go. And when he did – I swear I saw a smirk on his face. Then out of sight they were, gone for good as I climbed down and headed north on the highway, out of town. Feeling this time, a sure freshness of freedom.

As for any more running. I couldn't! I was tuckered out! My condition was rapidly deteriorating...

I'd have to take cover in the nearby ditches whenever a car came by. Then once it was gone! I'd strut myself back up on the highway and head for homeward bound.

It was a slow process. being so tattered and Battered, I could see way up in the distance (a) beam of rays – glowing Hoping it'd be a closed gas station, most gas stations were leaving their restrooms open for the public.

When I finally reached its sight spread across the midnight blue I came upon a drive-in. I began to receive the wildest stares, I knew I'd have to do everything fast.

Reaching the restrooms, you wouldn't believe what I saw!

Upon first notice, was my hair. It was bunched together in one matted mess – complete with sweat and blood.

My face. I could see whiplash lines across my cheeks and forehead by all the branches.

Lordy, My arms, Front, Back, and Legs were scratched, scraped, beating bloody and blue – from the gouges off of the razor wire spools.

I know I had to get with it though and move fast. I started hiding in one of the stalls and proceeded to wipe the blood off my torn-up body. Changing clothes wasn't easy.

I could hear girls coming and going when suddenly I heard this soft voice whispering at the door asking if I needed any help. And then proceeded to ask me if I was from the school just a mile down the road; "Me and my boyfriend want to help you out. My niece was in there. We will take ya anywhere ya need to go."

I was so grateful, as we split—with a cop being seen passing as we left...

I wound up spending the night at their place being that she was a nurse, and him a firefighter. I was. Awestruck too all over again.

A guardian angel perhaps?! As I then immediately thought of Mom.

The next morning, as they said they'd do, plans were on the way to drive me into

Troy, a good 75 miles away. She was determined I'd receive a tetanus shot.

I was then on my way home – Just as happy as a lark feeling now free as a bird.

Only to then be home free for a while from this wicked School, full of haunt left in reserve.

To make it a bit shorter towards the end here. I wound up gone for 3 weeks, then busted, only to be sent back to Adrian again. My counselor. cut a deal with me and said "If you don't (run) and do a full 60 more days (without incident) we'll let ya go."

I excepted her offer.

As for any more spooky experiences. No ghost showed up. But the sounds off the walls and doors in the halls kept banging.

Then after 60 days, arriving in Dad's maverick was Keith and Lori to pick me up, and off I was to a party once we hit Troy. Weeehooooo. And so goes the story of Adrian my friend, of a school that was full of spooky surprises. The End. Love, Aileen.

Scars

As horrific as it was, with me still at 15 and scarring me up pretty bad (Because of all that barbed Wire) seemed only a wee pack of a punch to all the massive amounts of blows I'd receive and be shocked with the rest of my life.

I mean Rape. Gang-raped. Getting pregnant. The unwed home. Adrian. Scarred by fire. Scarred by barbed wire. Man. What next?!

First Real Relationship

Say do you remember a boyfriend I had back then that use to hang with me at the pit? Bobby Rowland. He had Beatles styled hair blond, blondish red mustache? Curious. He was my first. While I was at Adrian he overdosed on heroin. Died.

Bobby had Blondish/Brown long hair almost to the shoulders, and a blondish/Brown mustache. around 5'8" then, always wore a leather jacket.

My nickname was Apple as a teen. Bobby my teen boyfriend gave me the nick. When I met him he wasn't in any motorcycle club, but along the way of our dating and partying in all our puppy lovely stuff he joined them. Anytime I met a member of the club they'd call me Apple. Bobby overdosed on heroin and died when I was in girls training school and I was lost in love. My luck always dies out doesn't it?

Chapter 3. Life On The Run (Age 15-16)

Friendship With Dawn

After my stint at Adrian, everyone started to go their separate ways, Delia, the mayors' daughter began to fade out as well. Only for a new gal to come in and take her place in hitchhiking and partying with. Her name was Dawn.

She moved from Hazel Park to Troy about a year earlier and was just getting herself known around town and in school when I bumped into her out at the pits. (an area of 3 man-made lakes near our neighborhood and in doing so would become an everlasting friendship. Which to this day is still going strong.

Personnel note; Thank you, Dawn. Love and Loved ya like a sis. Linda and Laura too.

But for Delia and I's hitchhiking, there was a bit of difference with Dawn. We didn't hit parties as Delia and I did but instead headed out to parks to cop drugs for personnel use or to sell. Or we'd head out to the mall or the race track "to panhandle" and then hitchhike back to the park to buy some more drugs.

But best of them all was, The Hole and the Pool Hall located in Rochester Michigan, These 2 places were our favorites. And if you wanted to find us, normally you could there.

Now "The Hole" was a bowling alley located underneath Rochester Movie theater. It was nick-named this because of the few lanes it had. Which had like only four. And for a pastime and a little quick cash, a lot of us kids would set up pins for 75 cents an hour. Because ½ the time their machines wouldn't work to drop the pins back down. So they hired us to manually do the job as we'd in the meantime, get high and secretly sell drugs in the place, chuckle.

As for the "Pool Hall," it was beside the theater. Another favorite of everybody's. I'd learn to shoot exceptionally well – the game. So dam good It'd later be used as a tool to hustle with. Especially while on the run, when needing food or a room for the night. Making 50 cent Bets or a dollar on the game, and rarely ever losing.

The theater we hardly hit. There were too many other things to do! But as a youngster, I can still remember the prices for the few times we did see a flick there, with coverage, a quarter. And a box of popcorn only a dime.

Nothing like the good ol' day's ay?! For sure.

As Dawn would become a wonderful friend, I'd come to find out her parents were cool, with two more kids in the family, Billy, and Don.

And since Dawn, Ducky, Keith, Lori, and I were all the same age we all fit in well together as a group to goof around and party with. And that we did. Starting at the pits.

These pits we hung out at consisted of three man-made lakes that were nestled deep in the middle of the woods of some 435 acres running alongside our neighborhood. Man talk about kick-ass! It was Helter Skelter.

So we kids were left to the pits to run. Be it to car racing or dealing drugs.

Yet as each party rolled away, winter rolled in to quell the raucous we revved up.

The Hippie Aesthetic

Haha I'm at the point now in one of your letters about cleaning the house and running into some old clothes at least 20 years old now and might just be back in style today. Hahaha for real.

Have you seen the tight tie-dye shirts or the hip-hugging bell-bottoms they have out today... if I was out shopping with ya, I'd be picking up some of those stone-wash straight-legged jeans with the studs on them. As well as some T-shirts with Zips or pullovers. Definitely cool looking in my book.

I can see ya now. Just as clear as day at 15 with your old hip hugger black bell-bottoms, and pull-over halter tops you loved to wear. Black hair down your back with your muscle-bound look, always challenging someone to arm wrestle at the kitchen table, while the music played away in that small living room you guys had. Sneaking the cigs and booze and partying up there whenever your parents went away. I remember how bad I wanted those black jeans and how bad you wanted my brown fringe rawhide belt. I think we eventually wound up trading off. Chuckle. Chuckle.

We did have a lot of fun together. I remember taking you to the race track. or you coaxed me. But anyway. Remember how I taught you to panhandle. We made out pretty good too. Didn't we. Remember our bell-bottom pants.

Wheewhew and when studs came out. Lord, we started to stud everything. I remember your black hip-hugger bell-bottoms you loved to wear. And you studded them up the leg. Then Ducky fell in love with them. And put them on. They were really tight. and a bit short on him. But he still wanted to wear them. And if I remember right. You'd both always fight over clothes.

Keith's Crush

Dawn. About Keith having the hots for ya. He did! At first. Then that feeling passed away and all it was was a sisterly thing. The hots came where you guys first met. But, when he found out how tough and tomboyish you were, it all melted away into just one dam good friend.

The Clark Gas Station

The Clark gas station! Boy, look at it now! Jet set Ay?! hahaha. And I bet the bathrooms are thoroughly in order, as in our days they were as crappy as a shit house in the backwoods somewhere! hahaha. Today to drink in the bathroom before heading out somewhere to raise hell, we'd need "Champagne" to go with the flow of this jet-set! hahaha. Wow, plush isn't it?...

The Alibi. Oh man, they really decked it up didn't they. Super! And yes their pizzas were so juicy, just the right pepperoni grease taste and cheese on. I loved taking you there and getting some with that hooker money I made. Hahaha, now don't feel bad. It was good sex and good food too. So I can't complain. Only the bad and hairy times I had with men. I wasn't always hooking though. I also won the bread and butter pool hustling. I remember trying to teach you how to shoot. Good Memories. For Sure.

Painting Dawns' Bedroom Black

Do you remember when you painted your basement bedroom?! Black! Hahaha. Then one day you and I did some orange barrel acid. I was up lying on the top bunk, and you were lying on the bottom. We lay there just explaining to each other about our Kaleidoscopic high. Plus other stuff. We had a blast. For now Love Aileen.

Happiest Childhood Memory

Dear Dawn, I finally looked up the word to spell it right. Let's "Reminisce"... "To discuss or think of the past" hahaha. What's this C in it. The way I spelled it wrong looked better! As I spelled it "Reminess". OK OK OK so the C is silent. Then what the hell did they even put it in there for?

Man! So let's go back to the 70s buddy. There we are smoking a doobie out of a 4 finger 5 dollar bag of black gungi I copped through some guys from Clawson. Where, at the pits and waiting for the rest of the gang to arrive, from their we're going cruising in Lori's New Port. Remember that black tank?!

We're all getting stoned and as the radio plays those good ol' tunes, we rap on places to go and where to eat and cop some mesc or anything. We try woodland area, we head then out to Stoney creek. Nothing.

Then to some parks. Still nothing. Last resort the mall. 15 mile and Jimmy E. The Bizarre shop! We finally cop. Then off we go for more cruising. For the store and booze and then were to settle and enjoy our high. Where else but back at the pits.

Later boredom strokes and we've got to head out again. So we go to the pool hall. Not everyone has the quarters to play the game. But I do! She works hard for the money! Ba do do do Ba Ba Bingo! Here's a little chink for you Keith, you Lori, and of course my friends in need. No biggy! The bucks are easy to achieve hahaha.

Feeling Like Lori Stole Dawn Away From Her

I'm reading about Lori and you back in our kid days. Well, give me a break! You say here; 'you and Lori didn't hang all that much around together'. Sure you didn't. Lori scooped you up and away from me. I was 'pissed' and that's when our friendship faded. Now you can say 'that's not so' all you want. But that's how I remember it, Dawn.

Ending Her Friendship With Dawn

The last time we saw each other was Keith's funeral, but our last hang out together was a snowy day, cold windy, and wet, when all my 45s and other personnel belongings were trashed out at an apartment. Yea! that set me off! That was the day I decided I never wanted to see you again. Sorry, But it's true.

This is Dennis who was also homeless as a kid & built a fort which them and Aileen slept in to stay warm.

The Pits

Nick Broomfield Interview

Nick voice-over: We went to visit Dennis Allen, who lived with Aileen in the woods and now lives in this house,

Nick: Hi, how do you do, I'm Nick

Dennis: Dennis

Joan: Hi, Joan.

Nick: And who are these fine creatures (pointing to the canaries)?

Dennis: Freckles and Freda

Nick voice-over: Dennis looked up his only picture of his time in the woods with Aileen.

Dennis: In fact, the police took this picture, that's how I got it, Nick: what's this of

Dennis: Well when they were subdividing, they through all the stumps over in one section, and this is all made with stumps, with straw packed in em, this is where I slept, just long enough to get in there and sleep,

Nick: So, Aileen would come and visit you?

Dennis: Yep every now and then, she'd come and find one of my camps. in fact, the last camp I was at when Aileen found me was, what we called the little round lake, it was way down at the bottom of a gully, ye know it was round, and I had a piece of plywood that someone had left there, and I just made a lean two, with two posts, and put that upon it, that was the last place, in fact, Aileen, last camp I had she came to, I had that one

Nick voice-over: This is a photo of Chief the local pedophile, he was rumored to be the father of Aileen's child, chief later committed suicide.

Nick: He was kind of a bit of a strange old man wasn't he?

Dennis: Yeah, people thought he was, but his house was a gathering place for kids, cause they had kids from everywhere that came there all the time. And I remember when I was little, see he'd wanna pick up kids and put them on his lap, and tell them stories of this and that, and I never would allow it, cause I just, he kind of freaked me a little bit, I can remember one time, he had some chicken eggs because he had chickens and all this kind of thing, and he'd pick em open when they weren't ready to hatch, and I couldn't stand it, him doing that.

Nick: He picked them open?

Dennis: He would pick the shells open, as they were trying to come through, and it would be too early for them still.

Nick: And they'd die?

Dennis: A lot of times they would, they weren't really ready to come out of there.

The Family Unit Was Gone

Our family was falling apart.

Mom was gone. And us kids left with broken hearts. While Dad was going off in a 90-degree turn for the worse, under his own crush and despair. Hitting not only one bottle of wine a day but 3 or 4. The man was turning himself a wreck! Causing then all of us to desire to run. With Keith going 1st, Me 2nd.

Our hideouts! Friends houses.

Yet friends weren't always available, nor could they always pull through for us on a place to stay. So if Lori couldn't stay with friends, then she'd usually run back home. Dad and her didn't have that much of a communication gap. As she'd likewise continue in school.

But for Keith and I. We weren't as Lucky. Both of us wound up in the woods. Quit School. Only to then eventually hit the highways of America. Homeless.

So it was a mess. Stuck out there in those woods.

I still can't understand the Hypothermia jazz people claimed one's to get if you're left out in the cold too long. Cause I slept in the freezing rain and snow and still didn't get any of this! Only to then have my butt up the next morning with me and a bar of soap, bathing away in the lake. Dutifully getting ready for school. Attending to cover up the run. While Dad kept to his word – he wouldn't call the Cops. And this time Didn't.

So I was left only with my school to worry about. As I'd gradually seek better shelter in other places than the woods, such as abandoned cars.

***

I wrote Linda & Laura today... also one to her Mom. Her mom is quite, tiny, and cute like my mom was. Real Serene, laid-back type. Is your mom like that?! I only remember her being at the kitchen table puffing on a cig and asking ya were you heading out with me. She didn't seem to mind our friendship. But I believe your dad did a little. I don't blame them. I was wild looking. Hippie to the Core. Wasn't I though?!! Beads Beads Beads! I believe I started getting you into wearing them.

"Say! you think your Mom + Dad would mind if I spent the night, tonight?! Man, it's gonna hit 40. I'll freeze to death." And I wasn't even using ya back then. Not in the least! Loved ya dearly!

Even after I couldn't stay over many times and had sleepless nights of cold, sleet, snow, and rain. Those were some ROUGH nights. And had many throughout my lifetime. It's like being a soldier/sleeping out on a battlefield. Only no gunfire, Just "Silence" you must at all times keep a keen ear on, in case someones coming.

There was a time I was sitting out at the pit. Oh, around 1:00 in the morning. Cops from Troy noticed me. Beaming their flashlights in my face, they asked who I was, what I was doing out here, and where I lived. Well, I was at the pit next to your house! Lights were still on at your place, and the porch light too. So I told them, my name was "Dawn Nieman" and I live right there! I'm just out for some fresh air. They asked me for your parent's names. Where did your dad work? Well, they left. And so did I real fast. Took off into the woods.

***

I did get the part slightly on Kim. What is this? Running away jazz! Listen, please! I remember winters when I was a runaway. Sleeping in the snow. No money, no warmth, nowhere to go, hungry as hell. I remember a time I awoke in the spring sleeping at the pit, (near Atkins) Raining like hell, plus thunder and lightning. I looked up and saw the hills sand turning to mud sliding down at me, and swirling mud around me. I was so tired, and weak from lack of eating. I said! Screw it, I'll go back to sleep Running away doesn't do anything but give you the freedom to turn wild. Burn your brains out on drugs, and, booze. Turn pregnant. Be an ass hole! And learn as you grow up. What a loser you were.

Lastly, besides hundreds of the hellish deals that I had to go through as a runaway. I remember a guy from High School offering me to stay at his place, since he lived outside of his parents' house, alone, in an apartment in Clawson. He got me drunk, he got me high. I passed out! He must have carried me to his bedroom. During my unconscious state friends of his, that some I knew some I didn't, must have started to come over to party. Apparently finding I was in the bedroom they all conglomerated a plan of raping me. They tied my wrist to the bedpost. Spread Eagle tied my ankles to the end bedpost. I awoke with cum all over my chest, face, stomach, crotch (stinky all over) mouth hurting. They must have forced head on me in my unconscious state as well.

When I screamed bloody murder to untie me. They did. I got dressed and said I'd go to the cops you scum. They told me if I ever did. Lori would be next, and/or your death And this was back in the 'peace, love, no war' era. Today is even worse. "20 folds over worse!" To them, I was 'a nothing'! because 'I was a runaway,' 'with no home'. Don't let friends entice you, Kim, to leading a life of meaning nothing that you'll regret. And take it from a pro! You just heard a "fair warning."

Nick Broomfield Interview On Being Thrown Out

Nick: But how did it feel like having to live in cars and in other people's houses?

Aileen: It was living hell...

Nick: Living hell...

Aileen: That's why I went to Florida, yea! I mean you know sleeping in the snow, I mean sleeping in snowy weather in a vehicle on cinder blocks at Richey's house! With no blanket, I think I had one blanket and one pillow, it's ice-cold outside. That's when I'm thinking I gotta go down Florida or something man, cause I was sleeping in the snow, out in the woods sleeping on the ground, in the snow.

Nick: You must have been frozen!

Aileen: I was frozen man, yeah! I still got marks from, my toes are blue to this day, my feet are blue, probably why my hands are like this, today. My hands are as you can see are like their frostbit looking.

Nick: And how were the other kids then?

Aileen: The other kids, they're all living in their houses (breaks up laughing). Well I was out on the street, but that's alright man because see I lived through it; I went down to Florida, because I could, started trucking all around the United States of America and stuff.

Nick Broomfield Walking Around The Pits With Dawn

Nick voice-over: After the baby Aileen became the local untouchable, she spent 2 years living in the woods at the end of her street.

Dawn: Aileen used to have a fort back here, as a matter of fact.

Nick: With Dennis?

Dawn: Yeah.

Nick: So, Aileen would just sleep Rough?

Dawn: she either had to sleep in the cars or go around prostituting at night to keep warm, stuff like that and hopefully she'd get a hotel. You know some of these guys would say come on, let's go get a hotel, then she could get a shower, that's how she'd wash and stuff like that or she would go to that gas station up there, which is still there, by the way, used to be the Clark, that's where we used to go up there and pinch our noes and drink, what was it?

Friend: Moonshine?

Dawn: Peppermint schnapps, it was disgusting, it was the only way you could drink it, get a quick buzz, I mean sounds sickening, it was sickening.

Nick: Must have been freezing in the winter?

Dawn: Yea well it was for her, I mean I didn't come out here in the winter for sure, none of us did.

Nick: She was out here in the winter?

Dawn: Yea it's why she left.

Nick: Did the other kids pick on her a lot?

Dawn: Yeah they always picked on her, or she picked on them. Cause they always had something terrible to say about her, but that's because she had a baby and they naturally assumed, well she did get, she slept with people for money and all that, so I imagine the girls in our days probably thought, well she sleeps with everybody, they just didn't like that.

They don't think it's funny now though, they think it's terrible the way they treated her, and everybody all of a sudden comes out of the woodwork and says "aw I was nice to her, and I gave her clothes," all kinda shit like that, no they didn't!

Drugs

The Head Shop

Say – do you remember somewhere on 10 mile and Woodward some head shop we all use to cruise through – looking for drugs or just to have a browse or steal stuff. Hey! I can't help it if I'm honest. Chuckle... Chuckle.

Anyway! Do you recall the floor-designed "Water fountain fish tank" deal they had? It was round, water running over rock as a water fountain deal – With fish swimming around there / open view – can touch fish deal – they set up in the middle of their head shop.

OK.! If you do.! Were you with us when Jenny Kerr – "drunk as hell" – fell in it. When we pulled her out. The fish was floating on top of the water – deader than a doornail – or knocked out
 royal! She was staggering away – all soaking wet – as we all gazed at the fish in Amazement – besides laughing our butts off.!

I remember Keith was with us, Ducky too, and they were just standing back laughing away. I was staring at the fish – thinking – geez! I hope the owners of this place haven't caught on yet to what just occurred, and that we need to split before we get kicked out of here. All of which I didn't want to happen – because I was hoping to cop some dope.

But if my memory serves me right – I believe we were kicked out. Jenny was too drunk causing a royal scene. I know you remember the theater, bowling alley next door below, and record shop above the bowling alley that was next to the theater, in Rochester. But were you ever with me – ripping off albums outta that record shop. There were pianos next room over. So I'd gather albums together – then roam over to the next room over and pretend to be checking a piano out! then I'd hide the albums behind one! Once I got enough – I'd put em under my huge coat. Never got caught. But my dad was picking me and someone else from Rochester, and I remember when I got in the car – my dad said – why is your coat square looking. I told him it was just the way I was sitting. acquired one hell of a collection – eventually. Poor Mom. Whenever she'd ask where I got all the albums I'd always say. "Borrowed" For now Love Aileen.

Selling Drugs

50 Bucks for 6 pills. Geez! Drugs have really gone up haven't they since we were kids! It used to be only 50¢ a hit remember haha?! And speed for a quarter hahaha.

Did you ever cruise with me to 10 mile and Woodward to the Zoo? I use to once in a Blue Moon back then, go there and sell. It was easy Just hitting the pavement and cat-calling drugs for Sale hahaha. The Woodstock days and early 70s were a trip!

I miss the hell outta our teens! But now that I've found the true meaning of this world's division of Good and Evil. I would love to walk through my teens, Same family – place – people – everything! but just much more cleaned up...

LSD

Do you remember 'window acid' LSD? Was so small, little crystal-like deal. Super hard to cut 4 way.

Did you ever go with me to the Amboy Dukes house on 20 and Rochester? They lived right next to the Clark gas station. Yes, good Buddy. The Amboy.

Dukes – the group lived there and I use to always head over to cop drugs and party. Plus spend the night over from the cold as a run-away! I hope you were introduced to them, and remember. They were the ones who sang "Journey to the center of your mind." I use to go over and watch them practice. This song was my favorite. Bob Seager used to live 2 streets down South or 20 miles from Hartwig. Vince Lawsons street...

Getting Caught Smoking Weed In School

"Can you remember the time!" Do you remember the fight me and greasy-haired Penny Dole and I had at the front steps of troy Union Grade School? Do you remember when Lori, + Ducky got in that car accident? Do you remember a guy with really long jet black hair named "black sheep" at the high school? Well, one day. He and I went underneath a stairwell near the new section they built that had swinging doors that head outside. Once you hit the bottom of the steps. Well, he had a 4 finger lid of "Acapulco Gold". we went under there to roll a big one and smoke it there. We heard footsteps coming down. But we figured that was just another kid on his way out to somewhere. So we finished rolling it. And started to lite it. And Low and Behold. It was the Principle. He looked at us both and said "Report to my office now" Black sheep. Gave me the lid. And he started up the stairs. I said to the Principle. Bullshit! I ain't reporting now where. Matter of fact. I quit school. Right now. He said. Then you get off of these school grounds right now Wuornos. And if I ever see you on them again I'll call the police. You understand hahaha! I walked out the double doors with the pot. And that was the day I quit school. What was really strange was that the principal knew I wasn't living at home. But in the woods. I guess he admired me, for having the guts to still go to school, as a runaway, and living in the woods near your house. A trip huh!

Crime

We were innocent back in our days, weren't we? The most our little horns did then... Well for me anyway was hmmm. Come on, Come on, Aileen, Confess. Oh OK, Gulp.

Threw toilet tissue up in a guy's widely spread-out oak tree. Threw green tomatoes at passing cars. Then older got real courageous and – B-B's/ out passing cars – Lying out in the woods off of 20 mile. Near the house.

Aileen! Why that was MEAN! I know. I know. I feel terrible today. So how about you. Lay it on me. And no lying OK?

***

Did I ever tell you what Heidi and I did in Apopaka Florida! Probably not. It's another criminal offense. A trucker with his little boy with him picked us up. He felt for us out on the road and offered a place to stay in Apopaka he had. He said we could live there if we liked – rent-free – as long as we cleaned it up, and did whatever else in fixing it needed. Young and dumb we thought it was a fantastic idea!

So the night was beginning to fall upon us. We fixed the bedroom up as best we could to prepare for some Zzz's. But as we were doing that, we found a huge rat in the bathroom toilet. And realized all the little things we were finding all over the floor of the house wasn't hamster food, of which it looked like, but rat shit!

The next morning we awoke to rat shit all over the blanket. They crawled over us throughout the night! Yuck! We were petrified and totally pissed off. Revenge was now settled in our hearts.

So what we did. My idea. Was decided to sell his furniture and kitchen appliances, and use the bread for food along the way up to Michigan we contacted a company interested we wound up getting 200 bucks in cash.

Needless to say. The trucker lost a Kitchen Range, a huge deep fryer, a refrigerator and the rinky-dink bed we slept in, all of which was new-looking, except for the bed.

One of the fondest memories of Heidi I can recollect. Although it was as juvenile delinquents.

Whistle!!! Lordy Lordy Lordy. God, please forgive me for this one and 100s of others. I ripped a guy for 200 and another for 4500. Then the 22 caliber rifle. Zip that was it.

As for the cases. Cars and jazz. That's different. I became possessed in the force of heavy beer drinking and bad experiences to recollect while under the curse of alcoholism. All so sad. But true. The real Aileen never killed anyone. I'm sure you know just what I mean since you have seen the real Aileen from years ago. And I'm back too. Only on death row. Had you of seen me in 89 an in this trance by the Devil you'd know I wasn't me at all. Something was wrong royal and something else was controlling me.

Well, it's time for me to close er up. May God watch over us at all times.

Take Care now,
Love Aileen.

Burning A Barn Down With The Gang

Dawn do you remember when the barn out near Attica got burned down. The matches and hay that were put together. All of us were tripping. We went to this haunted house deal. Where devil worshipers were once in a while using it to sacrifice animals. Anyway, it had a barn full of hay. I came up with a great idea. Since it was full of the stuff. To put matches in a line like a wick with hay. Then lit it. We took off. And about 2 or 3 miles down the road at a store we sat. Waiting for the outcome. And suddenly we saw the sky glow like mars was ready to come up from the horizon. If not. It's in my book. haha! I hope you do. We were stoned on orange sunshine and other stuff. plus beer. We had so much fun together. All of us. The gang. Certainly do miss those days. For sure!

We all just were out having fun as any teenagers do. Or did back then. Today the kids are really dangerous. That dam crack. Never tried it and Glad I didn't. Seems strange. Cause I've tried nearly everything. But I started to hate drugs. BAD! After 17 I gave up pot too. And from then on just drank. Period. Since then I've only snorted about 5 lines of cocaine in my life. And smoked about 20 joints. Zip! That's it. Nothing else. When I hustled I only drank beer. A couple times mix. But wasn't really too into it. Because when I was 21 or 22 I got hooked on white lightning for 2 weeks. Decided to quit. And it took me a month and a half to just get over the shakes from it. I realized then. the hard stuff wasn't worth it hahaha! I was a trip in my early 20s. Had a lot of fun.

Sex, Incest & Hooking Up

Incest

My Dad never ever sexually abused me, nor even exposed himself in front of me. If he did. He would have surely been locked up. Keith did have sex with me. But it was all mutual. Plus we were so young around 9 or 10. Also, it was basically for playing. Not downright intercourse. If they'd just ask me I'd tell them everything, so truthful. But no one wants to hear this 'complete truth' because it isn't vile enough for money-making.

Experimenting

You kissed Derek Kolb? Scary! But that's OK. If I remember! But it's vague. I see us near a pond. We were fishing for polly wogs. In maybe 6th grade.

He's asking for a kiss. I say maybe. He lays one on me, an inexperienced one, yuk. He begins to play with my itsy-witsy tailgate + headlights. Curiosity is flashing, he whips his fly out on the rod. When I see how small the worm is I drop the hook and sink-er. No plucking, just a dunking.

Reputation

Do you remember my boyfriend "Bobby Rowland" I had? A big guy named Danger Dan. Dan came alone to the Hickory party. I called him up and he came running. Bet he thought. Pussy! But he didn't get any. No one I knew did. Why?! Because I was always afraid of them running and telling others they scored with me. So I only went to bed with "outta town boys." Bobby was from Royal Oak. So guys like High School, or any Troy boys/weren't even allowed in my box, only Rochester, Clawson, Royal Oak, anywhere away from ever knowing anyone we hung out with, so word wouldn't get out. That's why whenever anyone did say. I fucked Aileen, I was like You bold-faced Liar! Never! Now Mike Fairchild, Carl Maddox, and Jack West got a little. Real little, They were the "Only ones!" oh! Gordon Marks once too, and Ben Lloyd. But that was "it."

***

I see, Perry "Beard" was the creep's last name. I had consensual sex with him up in Ted's attic. He was terrible. Little pecker too on that jerk. So honey, you sure didn't miss anything with him in the back seat that night haha. And now confession time, who was it I had sex with in Troy? Well!

Gordon Marks, Mike Fairchild, Carl Maddox, Jack West, Derek Anderson. That's all! Jack and Derek were just once. Mike, oh about 3 times. Carl Maddox, lord he was my first, can't count them all. But good and full of fun. Gordon Marks was huge and oh about 5 times. Erm Erm Erm had to prime myself! What can I say! Teen urges! We all had 'em.

Danny Corwall

Nick voice-over: Danny Corwall, like many other boys in the neighborhood lost his virginity to Aileen, Aileen was trading blowjobs for cigarettes from the age of 9.

Danny: I was just heading over there to see who was there and I got up to the fort and the door was kinda closed, so I opened it up, and Keith and Marc had Aileen in there.

Lawyer: What do you mean Keith had Aileen in there?

Danny: Well they had here in there and you know she was naked.

Lawyer: And what was happening?

Danny: Well, Keith was having sex with her.

Lawyer: Did you stay during that?

Danny: Yes.

Lawyer: Did you ever have sex with Aileen again?

Danny: Erm, just that day.

Max Reed

Do you remember Max Reed? Took him over to my pad and we got it on. Buddy, he blew my mind. That guy had a club between his legs. 2 1/2 inch circumference by 12 inches.

I bet you're like "Did ya take it all. Did ya take it all! Aileen. Tell me! Come on."

Me: No

You: Come on Aileen!

Me: Oh okay. No! I held it with 2 hands while he pumped. Honey, it was too big. But oh was it good. Mmmm. drove me to oz. WhewWeeeee, funny Aileen.

The Boyfriend Who Shamed & Bullied Her In Public

Nick Broomfield: Jerry Moss who was a lover of Aileen's, pretended in public he didn't even know her.

Jerry: She wanted us to be boyfriend and girlfriend, in public.

Lawyer: When you were in public around the rest of the kids, how did you act?

Jerry: Like she was nobody like she was dirt like I had nothing to do with her.

Lawyer: What would you say to her?

Jerry: Get the fuck out of my face, and go some fucking place else.

Lawyer: Did you call her any names?

Jerry: I'd call her ugly, bitch...

Lawyer: If she was following along behind you what would you have done.

Jerry: I dno, if someone was with me I'd turn round and throw rocks at her and tell her to get the fuck out of there, go home.

Lawyer: Why would you do that?

Jerry: Because I didn't want to be seen by her, didn't want to be associated with her

Lawyer: Do you know whether she was having sexual relations with anyone else at the time?

Jerry: Yes I did.

Lawyer: And who was that?

Jerry: Erm, her brother Keith.

Lawyer: Is that her uncle or her actual brother?

Jerry: That's her actual brother.

Dawn Expressing A Common Ignorance Of Gay Or Bi People At The Time Which Explains Why Aileen Didn't Date Women Until She Was 29

Nick voice-over: Dawn insisted that gays hadn't been invented when she and Aileen first became friends.

Dawn: They weren't invented, or whatever, there were no gay people.

Nick: Well what were they all doing?

Dawn: They weren't gay, there was no such thing as gay.

Dawn's friend: They were in the closet.

Dawn: No they weren't, there was no such thing, I don't remember a single person at school who was gay. I didn't hear this gay stuff till 10 years ago, well maybe 15, it's just now starting to be this acceptable haha, but no, there was not. Were there gay people when you went to school?

Nick: I'm sure that there probably were, I went to a British all boys school, there were many. That's where it was invented, us and the Greeks.

Dawn's friend: No way? Really?

Nick: Yeah, of course.

Protective Sister

Going way back to the bar David took us to I remember when he gave you your first kiss. I was scarred for ya. Cause I knew how guys were So I believe I got mad about this. Sorry if I blew that night of fun a bit. I was so lit, I barely remember all we did. You know me I always got blitzed being so free too.

***

Remember stealing gas from the rich neighborhood near your house for Loris Big Black Crysler Newport haha. We wanted to cruise around. So we did! Roomy too! The entire neighborhood gang could fit in it. The Troy gang! Owners of the Pits. at least that's how we felt.

Tom Case's Parties! I can still hear the stereo playing and see all the cool looking blacklight posters. Can't you?! Boy them guys didn't like me! At all! I was soooo protective of Lori. Wasn't I though?! But that was because some guys we all knew threatened me they would rape her. Guys! DO NOT, I repeat, DO NOT care about girls, the basic majority would rape a girl if they could. Well, time to get ready for our visit. Love Aileen.

Sex Work

No one, I repeat, no one ever got in my draws for cigarettes. I ripped off cigarettes from gas stations or bought them through hooking chink. Change from the wad of bucks I made. But I fucked No One for cigarettes. Geez! I wasn't that hard up! Stealing cigarettes was easy! And besides, if I was going to choose to fuck for something back then, since I was underage, it would have been for a case of beer or 2, or liquor before a pack of cigarettes or a carton.

Other Jobs

Cleaning Houses At 15

Remember when we use to work for 100 or 180 an hour. I worked as a maid, the "Rochester Motel" for 75¢ an hour. No kidding was around Oh 15½. Only worked for about 2 weeks. Some guy at the motel turned me on to 50 bucks for sex. And that did it for the slavery job. hahaha. I believe this is where hooking began. Realized I could make dam good money to help myself in my homeless state and took it up Do ya blame me!

Busking in Detroit

You're now talking about the Zoo. Well by George, this is where Kitty and I went to sell drugs during our high school days and skipping classes. Do you remember Kitty Howard... Let me tell you a story about her sister Sara and me.

We hitchhiked out to Detroit to look for some mesc. She decided she was gonna take the guitar out there, and dance in the street for attention, to get hippies crowded around, and then seek any drugs we could once the stage was set and the lights on us.

Well, eventually lights came! Her dancing was so terrible, she apparently attracted the attention of more than just hippies. Here came the cops! They proceeded to ask us who we were, our ages. and here I was a runaway. Well, suddenly up pulls a plain wrapper (regular Vehicle) with 4 white coats charging out and grabbing "Sara"...

When everything quieted down. the Cop finally explained the situation. Sara had been institutionalized by her parents and ran from the place. Anyway!!! Every time I hear that old song from the 60s "dancing in the street." It always brings me back to mind Sara. Man... that day.

We've all done wild things in our prime while partying. This is what she was all about. Just getting crazy while being stoned, solely for laughs. Her parents thought she was literally crazy. I've met a lot of crazies in my 18 years on and off of the road. She couldn't compare. The ones I met were definitely dangerous.

Today I hope her life is straightened out and doing fine. The parents. Straight Jacket their ass to hell. Evil Fuck's.

Chapter 4. Life On The Road

The Hippie Councilor

Well, I was due for an overload. I'd become a ward of the State, Until 18. Yet Dad, all he'd say is "go ask her," as he'd hand me the address of a place that was located in Pontiac. And off I was to find out.

Summer had come and gone, and fall was coming in. And the Winds were whipping up some Cold chills, while I hitchhiked in the brisk of it all. Searching away for this place Dad gave me. and eventually finding the address, to be no other than located next to the juvenile facility. And in searching for her office, among the rows of many so conglomerated down the hall. I knocked, was Welcomed in – only to then be completely shocked to the 10th degree.

I stood as pale as a ghost I'm sure, as I stared in at this Lady who had to of been in her early 30s/ and resembled the singer Carole King to a T.

What knocked me back about five was the fact that the "Song" "It's too late" was dedicated by me to my mom – Just moments AFTER I was told she died. And after I was "This Song" came on next, which seemed a very appropriate title. To be then dedicated to my beloved Mom so dearly missed by me now.

I mean check it out!

The day she died, I was told she did (at the pits which was unexpected with me. I had no idea she was ill.) only then (out at the pits with the radio on) Have This song come on as I'd then spiritually dedicate it to her (as soon as I'd hear it) To then hitchhike to her funeral, only to next be busted for running away. Then from there, to be sent to Adrian for 6 months. Get out! Only to then find out I'm now a ward of the state until 18. Next, be given her address of this counselor to see until then. Hitchhike out to her address and see her, only to then step in her office and stare at a woman who resembles the singer of the song I dedicated to my mom, just months ago. Awesome!

So needless to say, I was blown away! And then to top it off, I'd come to find out she even played a three-legged grand and sung like her too. Besides smoked pot!

Well, need I tell ya, We hit it off real good.

In the meantime, I was tripping out with a whole new crowd. Thanks to some guy who'd pick me up hitchhiking turning me on to.

The place was a Commune. Full of musicians, located just outside of Rochester Michigan. And they called their 80 acres of rolling hills and beautiful trees. "Teiken Farm House".

Around 30 people lived there. Male and Female. And with all that musical stuff, I must say I was in 7th Heaven. And all my childhood dreams flashing before me, as I dreamed of being a rock star. Well, let me just tell ya it was blessed. Wonderful moments shared.

Yet not only was this, Awesome! but I was likewise being introduced to some new drugs flowing around. Such as frog acid and Black gungi. And with these connections on the block, I started sharing the quality in high School and downtown Woodward in my small-time dealing ways on the side.

And then it wouldn't be long and sadly the Farm House would be sold as everybody was packing up and moving out.

And so there went the Commune.

Yep! All because of them I was now wearing love beads and putting embroidery on my jeans. As well as sewing on "Slogan Patches" all over my Jackets.

Such as zig-zags, peace signs and marijuana leaves. Just to name a few. And hitchhiking!

Man. It was the thing to do! Even songs were out grooving to the word. While I was turning quite a pro. at it, having started at 13.

Anyway, it was a nice day to thumb back to see her, the counselor lady. Even though it was probably 30 degree's out with snow all around. The sun was shining making everything as pretty as a picture on a postcard.

Pondering away as I enjoyed the scenic cruise in each car and thinking just what I was gonna tell her, as I hitchhiked out to her place. All of which looked like a Hippie's pad. Full of oriental rugs. Curtain beads. And incense always burning.

Well, let me tell ya I wasn't surprised that she didn't care about the fact I ran. Nor of the idea about school. But what I was surprised about was her willingness to see me through it all. Be it so she could make sure I'd never go back to juvenile or Adrian again.

She'd fix me up really good with a shower, only to relax next with a bowl of pot, music, and good home cooking. Boy, could she cook too! As our conversations stayed on home and school with problems and solutions. All of which only came to conclude. that the need was to leave Michigan.

By leaving Michigan, crossing the border would surely then eliminate "Ward of the State." As it likewise eliminated my need to wait until 16 to quit school.

Then Christmas came along for the usual commercialism with her and me both knowing I needed clothes. So she decided to charitably spread a bundle for me to receive a new look, for better rides.

Man. I lost my beads, bandannas, jewelry, fringe jackets, and slogan patches. You name it! All was over with. Even possession of drugs. And with shopping all done, next on the list was "Wait." I'd have to wait the Holidays out. Just one more sacrifice I couldn't stand.
January 2nd would be the date chosen to leave the Big Mitt behind. With Florida on my mind. Knowing the snow was getting too much for me to handle.

I cruised over her house hitchhiking again.

And once I arrived she kept asking if I was sure I felt up to splitting. As I reassured her that today was the day. There was no backing out now! Not with just an abandoned car to call home, buried in snow. So we packed in the car and off we were.

Man. I remember it well. Close to a whiteout, but we kept going.

And finally reaching Toledo, she parked where we thought was best, as the hardest moment of all came. Saying goodbye. Not only to her! But to Michigan and all the rest.

Stationed on the side of the freeway now we seemed to stare at each other as if to get our last pictorial in memory, then began to hug and couldn't stop! Boy, I was gonna miss her along with everybody else. While the tears fell to freezing it seemed.

But before I'd step out for good and be gone on a long journey of some 1200 miles or so to Florida, she wanted me to receive one last gift before I did.

80 Bucks.

I was hesitant. Man, she'd done so much for me already! I finally gave in and accepted it. Man. She was primo people. That's all there was to it.

As I placed my suitcase in the snow near my feet and pursued to thumb.

Full of anxiety now to greet what lied ahead. Yet not fully knowing that with the good came likewise The Bad and the Ugly.

Oh man was it cold. No gloves, hands red from the bitter wind, and no long johns as my jeans became frozen by the wind-blown snow sticking to the fiber. It took a good 20 minutes before I copped the initial ride to experiencing this new freedom. By A trucker heading out to Tennessee.

He was a good soul. After leaving me in Tennessee and advising me that I should head out to For Lauderdale Florida where all the teenage runaways hung out and helped one another, I did just so.

Upon arriving around 1 or 2 in the morning, a state trooper in his early 30s approached me for an ID check. I had no ID on me but gave him the works he needed in checking out my background. I was clean. At 16. Shew! Was my first reaction, and 2nd Thank goodness.

He then wound up talking with me, knowing in the process I was fresh to the area. and as A new kid in town. He wanted to help me out. or so he said. so he was going to put me up in a motel for the night.

All motels said vacancy, but each time he came out, he'd say there wasn't any. Eventually, he conned me into crashing out in an abandoned house outside of the beach area, near Dixie Hwy. Once there he showed me/by flashlight/around this dilapidated hole, and amazingly it had cold running water. Other than that, only a mangled joint with a mildewed mattress in one of the rooms.

He told me that he'd let his other fellow officers know I was here and not to bother me, and that he'd check in on me, just to make sure I was OK. I was grateful, and he left. who knows how much time passed as I was sawing logs, but suddenly here came blonde head – with his long flashlight in my face still in uniform, the conversation was quick and simple, stating he brought some of his buddies over to meet me, and not getting into a most humiliating and utter devastating event, I was gang-raped by his ass and other officers in uniform.

Living In West Palm Beach

After this ordeal, they warned me to keep my mouth shut, that I was lucky to be still alive and to leave fort Lauderdale.

I did, winding up in West Palm beach some 50 miles north of the area. Stayed there in West Palm oh a good 4 or 5 months with a guy named Cat. Once Cat left me to head out back to his ex in Albuquerque New Mexico, I headed out West and wound up for the summer in Sedalia Colorado, liven up in the mountains of with Sam and Rose Stone.

Living Around Celebrities In Palm Springs

You know Bob Hope's about to go! He's hospitalized for something right now. 97. Wow Ay! I remember as a kid. Around 16½ or 17. Hitchhiking in front of his place, there off of I think highway 15, in Palm springs. And there was this Super X shopping center which when I stepped in to get something, the clerks said I just missed Lucille Ball. That she was checking her out not 5 minutes ago! Then as I hitchhiked in front of Hopes house that looked like a huge Silver covered dome, I swore I witnessed Phyllis Diller passing by me in a white Corvette. So that was a trip. Hope was probably having a party.

The Commune in Colorado

Now here was an adventure to express in the complete fulfillment of utter joy I felt. I had a ball up there. Man, let me tell you. A blast!

It all started with being picked up outside of Denver heading south on I-25 by Sam, who was studying to be a certified electrician. He offered me a brew and then asked me if I was a runaway. He was so cool, and kind, I laid my recent history on him. He told me he wanted me to stay with him, his wife, and their 9-year-old boy named Peter. At first, I was like, no. I need to check out the states and sightsee. Then on second thought, I agreed.

He lived up in "Sprucewood." some 30 miles up in the mountains from Sedalia. I started to fall in love with the creator and his creations.

As time passed by in these Colorado Rockies, I would soon learn much from these mountainous gypsies who loved cribbage (the card game) and having hootenannies night, (singing in a group and jamming out with all types of instruments).

Rose would walk me through the wilds and teach me about land animals and shooting. Shooting from a 357 mag. as well as a 15 shot Winchester and even cross-bow 80 lb pull.

There were times that Rose would take me to the only bar up there around for miles, to shoot some pool. there I was a 16-year old kid with a non-registered gun strapped with rawhide around my leg from the bottom of the holster, shucking balls around the pool table like Annie Oakley. Loved it!

I was then handed a key to a storage shed, and campsite combined, for 10 dollars a month. (Electrical bill). (One light bulb/inside.) located just down a ravine from their cabin...

Back In Michigan Briefly (Aged 17)

I'm back Memory Lane still cooking good! When Ducky and Keith came over to my boyfriend's house where I was living, I had an 8 week old Alaskan husky, who I named "Rocky".

Rocky blew Ducky and Keith's minds. He ran all over the house like crazy, then I sat on the couch and rocky comes up to me like "gr" on his ass he sits, and like looks at me, (wagging his little tail) OK. Momma what command do you want me to do now. I had just gotten the pup a week ago for 5 bucks. I was about 17 then. This is when I came back from Colorado to Michigan for about 1/2 year, then split again to Florida. Well, my living quarters went, when the girl I was living with decided to use the stove as a heater and ran up a 240 dollar monthly bill. Back then 85-90 bucks a week we only made. I moved out to Detroit. That's where I met Gene Lewis, my 2nd real boyfriend. A bass player of a group named "The Brothers," later changed to 'The Concrete Birds.' I quit the factory job. Started living with him. Training to be a vocalist for his group. Now I must stop. Long, Long story. It will all be in my book. I just wanted you to know about "Rocky". What a smart dog.

Back On The Road Again

Finding The Dismembered Body Of A Woman

Fall was coming along now of "73" – With me just outside of Chicago – this time off an interstate called I-80, heading towards – Detroit. I came across a foul odor coming out from under the bridge, only to sit next to a viaduct full of red. Now at first, I thought it was paint – yet upon closer examination, I could see it was more than just that, but blood, while my eye's trailed up to where it was coming from, only to then see something bundled up in blankets between bridge and cement, as the traffic just whipped by without a care in the world to anything that was obviously very visible.

So with all of that, off I went to inspect. Looking around then for something to poke it with, and in finding a stick nearly proceeded up this blood-soaked slab of cement, as the stench only got thicker and thicker. So much so it started to burn up my eyes, nose, and throat.

Yet up I continued until I reached its bloodied bundle – full of maggots and flies. And as I examined its shape wrapped up in what appeared to be several blankets, it seemed to me to be that of a female with her head, arms, and lower limbs missing.

Well, I tell ya, through a combination of things, the smell, the horror, the fear, the flies and maggots, besides all the rest that came with it, I wasn't up to unraveling the blanket to find out any more of this sick scene. So on I headed down now to look for a mile marker or the exit sign to give a trooper the location if I could just flag a trucker down to get them to get on the C.B. to give it. Be that of Channel 9, a station used by local troopers everywhere.

But, boy when the trucker pulled over for me, shit did he ever show a careless lack of concern. Telling me he had an overload that was way late, and so wasn't up to checking the bridge, to see if all that I was saying was ever to be true or not, stuck there under that bridge to rest. And neither did the trooper when I finally got a hold of one on the C.B.! Explaining everything to him seemed as if it were all a hoax as well. Leaving it then at that, her whereabouts and on down the road ever to wonder if he ever looked.

And so ends this shorty having run into that bundled up mess that no one seemed to care about, but me, at 17.

A Near-Death Escape With A Serial Killer

And as the days went on wandering on to nowhere, winter rolled in, and I was now 17 somewhere off a highway just outside of Louisville Kentucky when up pulled a van for me having a guy and gal in it. And as we cruised on with so many things said———I was offered another chance to get off the road for a while, and this time hopefully find a job. Carrying always that "Motto" to try anything once, so at least I could say I've been there and done that! Whether a lesson been made to gain the Wisdom or a sour note struck, for a grudge, remained to be seen, as I'd give it another try.

So I stayed with her and her Mom for a time, while we both looked for work. And not finding anything in Louisville, went then across the bridge that bordered with Indiana, heading over to Jeffersonville, leading then two topless waitress ones. How to be one wasn't much. Just had to put brown tape over your nipples ———then wear bikini bottoms———"and presto" you were in the biz. And if ya could entice the customers to buy the most expensive stuff you were tipped then by the boss himself!

And as we started to get the hang of it, I could see that clients were more interested in us than the drinks, always asking us out while I really didn't think much of it! Man———I just figured the guy was lonely———and just looking for a good time, like I was and looking for. So when asked out———I excepted.

Now this guy who asked me out seemed to of had an interesting background, running it quickly on me then (as a) 7th-grade school teacher who was as well a 3rd-degree Karate instructor [or so he said]. And with that, I was pretty much impressed and convinced that he was just one good Joe looking for a fun-loving gal like me to have a good time with. So off I was then with this guy in a pair of jeans – T-shirt – and boots with – spurs. we hit one nightclub after another way on into the wee hours of the night right on through to Morn, until the money ran out, and him bent on getting more from home.
Yet to do that would take us a good 50 miles outta town.

Arriving, I could see two other houses sitting right beside his, in the eerie dark, off a dirt road he was on, miles from the main. And throughout the silence in the dead of the night—had me pretty scared as I felt a bit uneasy now, as he opened his garage (push buttoned) then closed it back up once parked.

Then said———"Come on———I'll make you a drink while I get the money!" Well—I just didn't feel right about it, with the way the house was, so far off the road. So told him———"No thanks. and that if he didn't mind I'd just rather wait in the car, while he went for it." Well—that didn't go well with him at all—When he then grabbed my arm and said "you're coming in Whether you want to or not!". And with all of that said and done – shocking the shit out of me – knew I was in big trouble and needed outta the car – "Fast!" Struggling under the grip I tried to break free from it and hopefully open the door. But as I did———that's when he slapped me in the face "REAL HARD." Only for me then to try and hit him back———when things only went to worse with him on top of me now slapping at least a dozen times more.

I tell ya, I don't know how I broke free from this son of a bitch, but did, stumbling then outta the car looking desperately for an exit out, that's when I noticed a side door and took off running.

Boy, was I booking it too, slipping everywhere off the wet grass, only to quickly get back up and run like mad till I ran into a maple, one huge ass maple tree, he was right behind my butt and about to throw a kick to the chest. And in lightning speed, I could feel something like spiritual telling me to block the kick with cupped hands, and throw his legs up just as high and hard as I could. So in that second, did! And couldn't believe I did it, working well, as he then on the wet grass fell flat on his back, only for me to then quickly run up to him and start kicking him everywhere in the face. Kicking away, with even my spurs. until I felt he was down enough to then run to one of his neighbors for help.

The first house I ran to was straight across the street from his with all the lights on and it seemed as if someone was up and around. Yet no answer. I ran over to the other house with only a porch light on. And as I banged away on their door, an elderly woman came to answer it, only to then tell me she'd be right back and closed it up again. Man, I was blown away "Big Time!" because of the mere fact that when she did the guy was right there, where he could just get up and pick up where he left off. And then back she was with her husband this time, only for him to realize what was going on next to quickly usher me in, then and call the cops.

When the cops finally came the first thing one said to me was "man, I can't tell if you're male or female, this guy must have really laid into ya! I can hardly describe your face it's so swollen." So I handed him my ID and said "look!"

I found out I was some 50 miles outta town. I'd also find out the guy had been wanted for the murder of two teenage lovebirds who were both raped and killed, then put in a bathtub filled with cement and buried then in the back of another place he once lived in. Then to also find out he'd been likewise wanted for the beating rape of a fellow officer's daughter, who wound up so beat up by the guy, that her face couldn't even be reconstructed with plastic surgery, he crushed her face in so bad.

Then I could hear off in the distance, thugs with moans, as I then looked over to where he was up for arrest, and could see flashlight swinging, knowing clubs were too. When a cop then said to me "just ignore it!"

Only for me to scream back "I don't give a dam if ya kill him!" And started crying.

Well, needless to say, I lost my job and staying with the gal, only then to move in with a chick who ran The Outlaws. But, when she realized I just wasn't going to be able to find a job for a while and help her with any rent, out I was with my face, all black and blue.

Leaving me then forced to head back out on the road in this condition. And as I was hitchhiking out to Louisville a couple pulled over for me, thinking I was a guy who had been in a bar fight. Then when they found out I was female and all that, I was offered a place to stay. A good 3 weeks before my face came back somewhat enough to hitchhike in, then back I was out all over the roads of America.

Living with Hells Angels

It was Bakersfield California, thumbing through when up came along this guy on a motorcycle without a helmet and of all things wearing a ski mask.

I immediately thought what's this guy doing?! Is he fixing to Rob my ass or what?!

When he then asked me the usual. If I needed a lift?! Well, need I say, I was hesitant, with another worry on my mind, a carload of Hispanics cruising around giving me problems. So up went my suitcase, we were then on a hardtail bike that resembled the bikes they drove in the movies, like in Easy Riders. Minus the paint job, of the flag.

I'd later learn who I was on the bike with while being likewise asked if I'd like to stay a bit with one of the most notorious bike gangs in America. The Hells Angels.

Accepted and spent 3 days with his wife, kids, and him, who if I can remember right was VP. of the chapter out there.

The ski mask was worn because of a wreck he was in 4 years earlier.

This old lady tried to pass his chop, only to clip him in doing so. As the gas tank then exploded engulfing him full of flames, his hands and face. Really got it bad, causing him to become tragically disfigured. So much so he wears the ski mask, along with gloves.

And once he heard of my own fiery experience I faced myself in the face at 9, that was it, we hit it off well then.

The breeze was shot, along with games of pool. Chugging on the pitchers. with others coming in and I was introduced to them too. All of which went by nicknames. Such as Crazy Joe, T. Rip, Frenchy Foot.

Getting these real close-ups of their ways and the chaps they wore. (Chaps refer to the Colors on their jackets for club titles.) All of which theirs is the Winged Wheel.

They did their gig like the mob. Expand and franchised across the states...

Doing so in a corporate mob fashion. And covered it up with smooth operations to invisible to detect in the dirt they made.

Yet that wasn't all! They were building their image as the rough and tough that they wanted to be feared as up in the movie gigs they were offered in...

Along with copping a bit of sidekicks off of dirty deeds in pay-offs to bump off or whatever for the extra.

Yet between all of the 3 days I spent, much to my amazement I was never sexually harassed. Ever! It blew me back royal too, considering who I was mingling with.

So after 3 days, I was back on the road again thoroughly impressed with the opportunity. As they aired much kindness my way, that'd I'd like to say back; thank you!

Staying with celebrities

Say. Remember the song. Slow ride by Fog Hat?!

I was in my teens thumbing to Lauderdale when off of I-95 early in the evening came to this boss-looking vehicle – similar to this one enclosed. And guess who it was who picked me up!

Still guessing?! Good. Keep on for at least 5 more minutes! Aileeeeeeen! Geeeeeez! Chhhhhccchhhhccchhhh. OK OK OK OK. Turn the page. And don't get jealous.

It was. Lonesome Dave, Lead Vocals for Fog hat!

FOR REAL

He took me over to his place where he and basically all the band lived in Uno beach Florida. This joint was huge, like a mansion! I got so stoned with him I can't recall how long I stayed with him. But anyway the place was Al Capone's old stomping grounds. And it was specially equipped with a Helicopter landing on top and likewise came with some more mafia tricks of the trade, off the river it sat on an underground boat entrance.

And of course, I wound up going to bed with him! Typical! I couldn't help it, sis! The opportunity was there! And this was so Unique! Especially with a hot band as they were then! Couldn't pass it up. So I did. and god was he – Small! So tiny I couldn't find it!

That bad ay?! Unfortunately yes! Hahaha, it was soooooooo sad.

"Happy 4th of July!"

Driving Without A License & Skipping Bail

I wanted to finish with ya on the rest of the interesting event of Fort Lauderdale and leaving it in the 69 Cutlass, but Heidi wanting to stay behind. OK. So off we are back to Michigan in the car.

I don't think I had my license.

Here we were in Ohio now. seeing that the gas was nearing empty and we needed to piss and all. We got off the motorway to have a break.

Laney was gonna count out some bucks outta the Wallet. Buttttt Couldn't find it! Panicking – only to remember – It was taken to the restroom – and either dropped it in there or left it on the counter or something! And with the median being grass now – and in a panic – I went for a U-turn in it – to head back to that exit and the gas station John. hahaha.

Now a Cop on our ass, for U-turning. And I'm driven with no license. Soooo! Here come the sirens, as I pull over.

Explaining everything does no good. The Cop tells us to follow him. We're directed to follow the Cop into the building – to meet the Judge.

The Judge has sympathy and then fines us 10 bucks. But the problem. we still haven't any money! And by now. It's all stolen. So I tell the Judge once again. As he tells us. You got 2 hours to get it. The plan now is Western Union.

Well, then he leaves and for how long I didn't know, nor care! As I look at Laney in piss and fear. We've got to get out of here! So, I told her, I'm gonna go ahead and leave. and if we're chased Ill try to outrun them,

OK?! Crazy idea ay? See what desperation will do? Make you think the wildest. So, I cranked it up and started rolling to I-75. I could see a state trooper near one of the construction areas on the freeway. So I told Laney, hide down! Maybe with one passenger it'll fool this guy, encase he knows about us. Waiting for the bread or to the clink we go haha. So she did.

Dawn! I kid you not! I floored past the crew. The Cop looked. Shook his head and went about his business talking to another guy. I thought for sure there was gonna be a chase. But, no such luck hahaha! And on to Troy we were once again. OK, to be continued.

Her Brother Keith Dying In Hospital

The Last Time Aileen Saw Her Brother Before He Died

I remember the last time I saw Keith. Even though he had cancer. Was at your house in the basement. He went to a party and broke his leg coming down a step. His marrow was getting weak. I didn't witness this. I remember him telling me about it. The next time Id see him from this, was when I hitchhiked out to San Francisco, to see him at Letterman's Army & medical center. I got Lucky.

A construction worker gave me 100 bucks to help out on my trip to see him... so, I went shopping for some things to get him. I bought a wooden flute that was real gypsy looking, and the book chariot of the Gods. and a Bible. I didn't know his cancer note was the size of half of a football on his neck. So I was sad at getting him the flute afterward. Anyway! when I finally arrived at the hospital. I asked where Keith Wuornos was. So a nurse said. One's in room such and such over there. I said Thanks. Then proceeding. There were 2 guys lying in separate hospital beds, one guy had a sheet and blanket up to his eyes. So I said, "is Keith Wuornos here?" I'm looking for my brother. So the guy in the sheet up to the eyes said, "he went downstairs to shoot some pool." "OK, Thanks!" I said and started out, thinking in my mind suddenly, "heck! if he's shooting pool, he must be feeling OK. Great!" Then the guy said, "Aileen, come here."

Questionably I turned and said, "Keith?" He said, "don't freak out when I pull the sheet down." And as he did. He imitated Bugs Bunny and you know he can do him well, and he said "Ay, what's up doc?!" My eyes immediately filled with tears, as they widened to 50 cent pieces. The tumor was so huge on his neck. I kept telling him I'm sorry I'm balling my eyes out Keith, but man. This is really scaring me. He said it was the size of maybe a pencil head. But since he volunteered to be a guinea pig for them. They didn't cut it out. and it's grown some now. I flew off the handle and said. Who's your Doctor. So he told me. He said they keep telling him he has a 50/50 chance to live.

But he didn't feel so. So I said. I'll be right back. I want to ask him myself. He protested a little. But soon I was out the door. Asking the nurse. She said oh there he is now. Right down the hall. I hurriedly walked up to him. And said. What the hell do you think you're doing to my brother Keith Wuornos. And I was yelling. But I didn't care. He said. I'm sorry that your brother has caught this disease. And we were trying all kinds of experiments to save his life.

Bullshit I said. He's already explained the guinea pig jazz to me. Go on in there, as I was pointing to his room. And tell him he's dying. Man! You fucking bastard. I hope we get a chance to sue the fuck outta you. And turned around and walked off. When I got back to the room. Keith heard everything. But he didn't bicker on it. So I knew he was glad then that I told an army personnel off hahaha!

He said I know how you're getting your money, Aileen. I know you're hustling. And I want you to stop it. I'm leaving you 10,000 dollars in a beneficiary. I said I won't take it, Keith. I don't want your money...
I just want you to live. Anyway, I stayed three days visiting him. He said I was the only one who'd come to see him in nearly 8 months now. This broke my heart. So I told him. I'd come more often. When I could. Four months later when I was really doing good hooking, wanting to rent out an apartment in San Francisco so I could be near him. They transferred him then to Ann Arbor medical center screwing up my plans. So I hitched from Florida.

Now. Ducky, I think you, and others were dropping in. So I didn't have to worry about his spirits as much. I just thought I'd lay this story on you.

Many many of them. I bet you've got a lot of them too. So you see that's why I'm writing so much old friend!

Her Brother Barry's Torturing of Keith

Once again I want to thank you with all of my heart for having visited Keith and helped him as you did. I can't believe what Barry did to him. Sick Motherfucker. I can't believe you had to bring him a "Pillow!" My god was that bastard insane or what?! Had to bring my bro a pillow.

Barry also! Barry and Dad, man, it seemed Dad was the only one he liked outta the entire family! All of which had me always look at him like the womanizing pig he was. So when Keith became ill like that. I bet Barry thought this was a good opportunity for revenge. So he tortured him like that before he died.

They hated us so much in the family they wish we were dead. Well! Their wish finally came true, didn't it? I personally don't see any salvation in their bones either. So, whatever will be, will be. The future looks bleak you see, I'm sure it will be, hee hee. Hahaha whatever Jesus decides.

Man Dawn, what Barry did to Keith. Had I ever known this – I believe a barrel of a gun would have stared in his face before Mallory any day, I hated him before you ran me down on all this info, but surely you can imagine how much now. I'd reload and reload on his scummy fucking ass.

Praying For Keith's Suffering To End

Now some 3 days before Keith died, I had hitched off the road of my wandering around the US to see Lori. She picked me up and began telling me about Keith. How bad off he was and that he's at Barry's now, could die any day, had I only known I would have tricked in Troy, got a place and stayed with Keith as long as I could. I just never knew!

I asked for a flick of Keith. So I grabbed it, knelt down and began to pray, asking God to end his life, so that this tormented state he was in would end. I never let up on the tears. I couldn't, I loved Keith to the max.

The next day at noon, Lori came home from work. she said. Keith died this morning. I was shocked. Needless to say, I strongly feel my prayers on him were answered. During the funeral, I remember you there. I also remember how Lori, Erv, Barry, and Diane (our so-called cough cough 'real' biological mother, who we never really knew) all looked at me in utter disgust when I began losing it in tears.

Amazing! Here was my real blood brother, nobody else's real blood brother... And them looking at me as if I was crazy. Man. FUCK YOU!

Scattering Keith's Ashes

I picked up Keith's ashes, and some stuff he left behind then drove down to Florida and spread his ashes in the Gulf of Mexico.

Looking through his stuff I found a Bible, in it was two doobie brother tickets. And also a pamphlet on Jesus and if you believe in him sign here. His name was there. So cool! So precious.

Around a year later, the song 'Jesus is just alright with me' was playing on the radio, as I mentioned to someone how much I liked the song, but don't have any idea who sings it. Then I was told the Doobie Brothers. I went What!? Huh, man alive, that's probably why Keith left the doobie brothers tickets in the Bible! It blew me away. Keith, he was so smart and soooo coool. Good thinking bro. God I loved him.

***

Keith's ashes were scattered here in Florida on the pacific side. Around Stienhattache. "So I drove down. And as I followed to the end of this road, I reached an area desolate except for a small restaurant. With what looked like rocks turned into some type of shoreline wall. There I cried my eyes out and dumped his remains along that rocky wall. then just drove off – crying wildly out of my mind. Oh boy was I EVER!"

Blowing Through The Money Keith Left Her

Oh my god! Amy Fisher's some big wig now Ay?! Bigger than us capital cases. Well I'll be Darn On the program, yes that is "Disgusting" the families greedy like that. Yuck. I for one would never be like that. Wasn't even when Keith died. The 10,000 he left. I blew in one month to get rid of it. I just wanted him alive. But fate wouldn't have it.

Married briefly in Orlando, Florida (Aged 20)

You know Linda wrote and sent a Xerox of an old flick of me and Lewie (my X) taken back at 20 when we got married. Apparently, the magazine that copped the flick – Retrieved this source of material from the Daytona Newspaper, back in 76. Anyway. this flick was taken in the Living room of one of his condos. He had 7. And this one's called the "Atlantis" in Ormond Beach Florida. I know if anyone found out how rich this guy was. Having as well had 5 yachts in his lifetime one would say "You should've held on."

Well. The reason I didn't was because he was sexually perverted. Once we were married, when he felt full control, he began to air it. Only to refuse and wind up beating his ass hahaha. For sure. From one end of the condo to the other. He's lucky to be alive. Come near to killing him one night. Grabbed a 22 rifle, threw him on the floor, put my foot on his chest and the barrel of the rifle to his forehead, and said "I want a divorce within 24 hours or Ill kill you."

He left. I stayed 2 Weeks in the Condo. And finally, the divorce came through. Then left, hit the road, and went back to traveling the good ol' USA as I did from 16 up to 20 and running into him, marrying. He picked me up hitchhiking. But the Article of course lies, as we wanted it to, and says he picked me up from a nightclub I sang at. Yeah. Sang at! Hahaha. I don't have too bad of a voice. Wish it was true back then. May have hit the big time in Rock and Roll. Only to later most assuredly go into Christian Rock. Oh well. Enough of his ass...

Sex Work

Hitchhiking Hooking

Now I know you're saying to yourself, what about hooking. Didn't it embarrass you then or anything?!

Well Dawn, no, if you're thinking it because of the way I worked as a hooker.

I did it in a way that wouldn't embarrass me, using this hitchhiking method. See. This method first of all, with everyone passing ya by had them basically thinking. That's all you're doing?

So it's like all these 'guys' knew what I was doing! And that just didn't bother me at all! I was just one of the guys so to speak. And plus they were guys, who knows guys any better than me! I know very well how they tick. Having dragged myself through so many personalities and all. So having them eventually learn what I was really doing out there wasn't a problem. It was "Society" as a whole! So this "hooking" in incognito worked! When I headed back into town in Daytona. I kept it all under my hat. There wasn't hardly a soul that knew this was how I was bringing home the bacon. I could relax and not feel ashamed see! So it's different altogether from 'street hooking' and 'topless joints' with all the slut and trash.

The Beach

Boy do I miss the beach. The Sand. The Sun. The Waves. The Water. I used to sit out on Flaglers with the Bible, drinking up Soda's all day. My favorites Mountain Dew and Mellow yellow.

When I hooked I was real natural-looking, with my natural self. Only wore mascara. And just a hair of eyebrow pencil on my eyebrows. Only because the sun bleached them out so bad. And I wore basically T-Shirts, Blue jeans, and Tennis shoes. Like I did in my teens. Cut-offs from blue jeans for shorts. I don't get why these hooking broads wear high boots, mini skirts, fishnet stockings, and all. Man. It really cracks me up. It all looks so stupid! And all the guys I ever went out with, having met hookers out on the road said those kinda gals turned them off. They look stupid and into drugs.

Cop Stories

One girl I knew used to tell me how a Daytona undercover drug cop she used to date used to bring her a small candy bag filled to the top with cocaine. They're cops! They'll only get their butts slapped, and walk. I've only seen one cop go to jail recently for the murder of a business lady. A State trooper pulled her over. This same trooper tried to have me give him head in the woods. He pulled her over. Faked an arrest, handcuffed her, drove her to a medium strip on 1-95. Raped her then strangled her to death. Sick fucker huh! There are many more I know.

Here's a real doozie before I close! I was dating a couple of officers. This police officer, a john of mine takes me over to his house. He wants to watch a few videos of people having sex. OK with me! No problem! We watch a few.

Then he says; "Lee, you wanna see one that'll really trip ya?"

Me; "Sure!"

So he pulls this video out from behind the TV. There are 4 of his buddies in uniform.

Then he explains the 4 women are 3 of the officers' wives, one a girlfriend. And the department sheriff is there. The 4 males officers in uniform now, proceed to start corn holing each other in the ass. While one's screwing a girl. Then 2 are making out with each other. And next, it flicks on to the girlfriend of the officer and she's getting balled by the dog. I flipped out alright. I told him to hurry up and shut the tape off. Then I sat there with a drink in hand, guzzling down going 'oh my God'. And these are cops. Then he tells me he was the video man, filming the whole thing. I started to decline to date him. And finally, it was refusing to even see him anymore. Every time I saw the officers I just wanted to spit good hocks in their face. Sick animals! Well, see they're not like they use to be anymore.

Other Jobs

Working As A Topless Bartender

They had a company out in Daytona on Ridgewood Ave which I tried getting a job at, a long time ago and far away! And wound up instead getting a job as a Topless Bartender at a juke named Sam's. What?! Chhhhhh. Yeah, had to bend real low ya know, I was hard up back then...

So I for a while was a Topless Bartender. That is until "Bike Week." 2 creeps came up to the bar, Drunk Royal. Well recognizing there 2 like that I began to tell myself they're gonna have to be 86'd. So as I started to, one of them sloshed out of their minds said "bitch! I'm Mouse and this is my partner in the outlaws Motherfucker! Now if you don't give me and my pal here another drink we're gonna tear this bar down ya hear! Now get us both our drinks and shut your mouth!"

God! I was shell-shocked. Shitting purple nickels. Only 2 weeks on the job. And the first time I've ever been a Bartender. Man. I didn't know what to do! So, then I figured OK. Just to keep the peace from a riot. Give them their drinks. Then of course I had to call the manager, and he came in and took over. God was I embarrassed. I wanted to pound those 2 bastards in the ground if only I could! Had I have been the hulk I would of! Geez! humph. So. that was quite an experience FOR SURE.

Anyway! Such were some of my jobs in Daytona. As I was also a Topless dancer for one solid day. God that's all I could handle. I was full of shame and stage fright, Royal! Hahaha, Oh was I. I held on for an 8-hour shift. Got 80 bucks for it. And that's all she wrote. Chuckle. Chuckle. I quit!

Trying To Enroll In The Army

You know I missed getting into the Marines by 2 messily points on my aptitude battery test/ 40 was as low a score you could get and still get in. I made a 38. I was 20 years old. I was running down a T or F questionnaire and missed a box. By the time I realized it, I was some 15 or so questions down. Retracted by erasing all I just answered. Started over. So I lost out. the Marines was my last try. After taking all other tests for the Army, Air force + Navy. So I finally said "Foohey!"

Working As A Welding Inspector (Aged 23)

Say. I heard the minimum wage went up. I remember my highest paying job I had in—79—was. 750 and hour. I was a Welding inspector for bellows. These deals went in military stuff and even space shuttles, at NASA.

How I got fired was because I allowed the people welding – to skip re-welds. Instead of sending the part to them to do over again! I'd put the part in the – Meltdown box, to be remolded to a disc.

Someone got wind of it. Rand to the boss. And the next thing I know, I was called into his office to be fired. Darn! It was a dam good job.

Anyway! Surely if I still was at Belfab in Daytona, I'd be making 14 bucks an hour by now – ya know!

Alcoholism

Drinking Every Day

And sure hope none of you's had any terrible hangovers. I can recall some pretty hairy tricks to get rid of off the road. Lordy, I must have tried them all too. But only one I really liked. Alka-Seltzer. hahaha. But I can't really say if it actually worked or not because I basically got drunk every day! So by noon, I was back to a buzz on the stuff. I swear once I had one so bad, I didn't even feel human! hahaha. I couldn't wait to feel human again. hahaha. It was a Terrible Hangover. Big-time bad one.

Happiest Memories

Going back to the old days. The 'Good ol' days!' I used to watch Leave it to Beaver, Lassie, Bowery Boys, Ozzie and Harriet, Ed Sullivan, American Bandstand, Land of the giants, twilight Zone, lost in space, voyage to the bottom of the Sea, Bat Masterson, Wild West, Bonanza, Wagon train, I Love Lucy, Dick Van Dyke, Jackie Gleason, and so many more with even Lawrence Welk, because my Dad had it on whenever it was on. Both my parents were into waltz-type music. Mom would listen to laid-back stations with some of our music we were growing up with like Love 93 out here. Soft, smooth, and real mellow. A station I also listen to now because of the junk there coming out with today.

The good ol' days. Like the Happy days series, they use to hang out at the soda, shops, while we use to hang out at the mall, bars, and head shops. hahaha Learning how to shoot pool was fun.! For Sure. I grew up as a shark. I was using the talent I picked up for bread & butter when hustling sex would get old. I did real good. Once walked out of a bar in buffalo Michigan with 99 bucks. Played for some 4 hours at a dollar a game. Lost the table only once. For Real. Old raggy pool tables + sticks I played best on

Had a technique for beyond the pro-way. The by the rules in shooting was out. I had a way of my own and loved betting pool. Had a ball, but turned into an alcoholic, I began to love bars with a passion. The socializing and pool playing, getting slouched did me in. I was hooked on the suds up to my arrest.

Getting Raped, Assaulted & Robbed

The RAPES were the most difficult to handle. NEVER to get over one, driving me burning mad in rage. Enduring so many from 16 to 34. As most occurred on the road, finally to wind up in the Kegs, they powdered, 18 years later, with a gun.

And I probably said it before but will say it again. I always tried getting off the road. but to no avail, when 99% of everybody I ran into out there were men. And with only one thing in mind when it came to me. That was to use, abuse, then throw out.

Raped At Gunpoint

So let me get back to telling you about incidences I faced. Then you'll see what I mean about, psychological and physical defense.

So there I was in the snow again. a Peter built pulled over and I climbed in.

As it kept getting quite terrible outside. he was forced to pull over. Once we were settled to ride out this storm as such was surprisingly propositioned for a free be, as we did. Well, I laughed and explained that that just couldn't happen as homeless as I was, and in some royal need of some bucks, so that if he was willing to pay then maybe we could surely work something out. But if not, then sorry but forget it. he then told me to either get up in the sleeper for free or get out. Again I laughed.

That's when he whipped out this .38 telling me either get in the sleeper or get out... Now!

Or get out? I sat there stunned and was amazed he still gave me an option with a gun, being pissed too that another pistol has been put in my face again. Wishing I had one of my own now to whip out back at him. 16 or not! I was getting fed up with it and began to get out. But when I started out that's when his whole attitude changed like a bolt of lightning. Suddenly asking me not to leave & packing the pistol away.

At the time I knew none of these weapons as types. This would only, later on, be taught to me.

Then he started squawking; "you're a fool! You'll freeze in seconds as soon as you step out there!"

I laughed, then on a serious note mighty pissed said; "I really don't give a dam man! One thing I know is I don't put out for anyone unless they pay! And even if you did the way you acted on me. no dice. It's pay or forget it! Bottom line, man."

He started sympathizing and apologizing for the threats he put me through. Next taking out his wallet to let me know he'd run outta bread and needed to wire for more. And that lastly he was just horny as hell.

After listening to it all, I excepted his apology as I'd eventually wind up giving him some anyhow! Using the "Psychological Method" on him. With too many miles up ahead still before I could get outta this storm and away from him.

Yet I'd run into others where that wouldn't work. Or would come close to a situation that would fall apart. Let me tell ya about the time I was hitchhiking outta Lexington Kentucky.

I was dressed to the hilt for such weather. Putting on plenty of socks, thermals, boots, scarfs, Cap, gloves, besides the nice thick coat I wore. I was still too cold. Yet because of all the clothes I was wearing it was hard for me to cop a ride. Well, they'd say they couldn't tell if I was a Boy or Girl standing there. Well, I fixed that little number later on when I could get a hold of some cardboard and marker. Posting then across it Girl or the State I was cruising to while I thumbed. And it worked out well too.

And as the cars kept creeping by because of the slick of the road, some honked at me. I could see way on the emergency lane through the flurries flying around, the back of Semis tail lights. I then headed over to see if the ride was for me.

When I reached his truck, I must have looked as though I had shovels of snow thrown on me standing there thumbing for so long, and surely had the weather been different I would have refused this ride, because of his size. He was toooo big! At least 310 or 340 it seemed. I mean HUGE! So much so, for 16, it scared the shit out of me! But I was already in the truck.

Reaching his final destination I was then asked if I'd like to stay over as we started rolling into the outskirts of this City. It would've been nice but kindly thanked him and preferred to be on my way.

While he started on a sexual track with me that caused me to feel there was double trouble coming. I noticed him grab something from the door. A .357 Magnum. Glaring at me full of hate with it inches from my head. Saying; bitch I'm gonna get some of that pussy tonight!

I could see the bullets gleaming in the chamber. having had just about enough of guns being thrown in my face. Blew and yelling away said; Go ahead you Mother fucker! Go ahead and shoot me you son of a bitch! Shoot me – fucker! I ain't got nobody! No family! No home! Nothing Mother fucker! So go ahead, Man, Shoot me Son of a bitch! Go ahead and shoooot Meeeee Godddaammmittttt!

His mouth was left hanging as he held that gun to my head. Then he lowered it awestruck! And said as he put his weapon back into the holster that was fastened to the drivers' door.

Girl! You've got Brass! Brass Balls! Man I ain't NEVER! How old did you say you are?! Goddaaammn! Now that's Brass! As he just kept repeating it over and over, as I started getting outta the truck. Pissed.

I yanked my bag free then grabbed a piece of paper I had out of my bag, and a pen, then walked on over to the front of the truck to copy his plate down with him just screaming away how crazy my ass was, and me lifting up the piece of paper I now folded up real small and waving it in his face, said. I hope this is your ticket to hell. I'm heading to that phone booth and call the Cops!

As he started to leave calling me everything in the book as I called him the same right on back. As you could hear all his gears just grinding away as he hauled ass out.

I then walked over to the booth to take cover from a crisp breeze blowing as I sat on the floor of it and pondered on what next to do, having hardly a car go by.

Raped At Knifepoint

It was Winter, still being 3 weeks into my 16th Birthday, as another Semi picked me up. I was so frozen with a fear that always crawled up my veins of getting frostbit. Leaving my feet and hands to bearing frostbit scars, visible today, with these tiny spots full of purple and grey indicating I had some close calls.

And although the truck was extremely clean and the driver seemingly likewise, his person was full of debauch to the hilt. Incognito. Continually telling me not to touch anything in his cab. Strange. And that if I wanted to keep riding with him then I'd have to hide up in the sleeper to do so.

I thought he was full of bull, until he pointed to a sticker fastened, that read, no riders.

Having fallen asleep along the cruise, when all of a sudden I was jolted up by him entering the sleeper jabbing a knife to my throat as another assault was on the verge to begin.

It was an instant reflex of course to defend myself. So we fought. You should have seen that huge truck! It was weaving back and forth all over the place
which had me wondering why nobody was coming around or being concerned. Here he had pulled his truck. way off to the very end of the exit ramp.

And as it was going on he kept saying: "I don't want to hurt you, but if I have to I will!" While I kept pushing his hand holding the knife, away from my face, bitching royal.

I thought psychologically I'd win this one with a bit of a huff and a puff put into it, but there was just no way. He pressed it hard enough then to let me know he was willing to kill.

Man I tell ya. I'd really like to know just what the hell they've got down there between their legs that'd cause them to become so violent.

And in the course of it all, he kept threatening to slice my throat or choke me to death. So off-balance in his assault that he couldn't decide which he'd like to do.

And although I was pretty beat up. I knew that since he was "teasing" in the situation that if I kept my cool I'd walk outta it all. Alive. So cut with the defense and dropped myself to his level, as low as I could go. Using the psychological method now to keep from serious stuff happening, sexually. Only for it to assist me, from sodomy.

His imagination was running wild under his psycho craze of sexual rage. Pushing it way beyond the word exotic. Flat strange and fully retarded. Drumming up practically anything he could with his semen all over me. Insane! As he'd ejaculate and copulate to these continual orgasms just to spill it all over on me. Be it in my hair, my face, my chest, or my stomach. Anywhere he could! And forcing me to hold his cum in my mouth, slide it around, then swallow, when he said so. So he was insanely bizarre and sick, to say the least. But grateful his sick ass self erased any ideas of sodomy. I take it his ideas with the semen kept him from wanting feces on it.

Then to top off the humiliation that he wanted me to endure, forced me out of his rig right then and there at the rest area. Having to walk in front of all those people who could only guess what happened, which wasn't hard looking like death run over with bruises everywhere. And semen stuck on me from head to toe. Let alone the aftermath of it all. Having to hitchhike out from there.

It was awful! While I bet the only reason why he didn't want me to touch anything in his cab, was for prints. Surely perhaps having had other plans in mind, yet found me too fueled up for. So skipped the rest in mind. All of which has me wonder then if my psychological and physical method worked after all.

Getting Assaulted by Strangers

And mustn't forget the time I was outside of Georgia this car pulled over for me, having the driver next only to backhand me square in the face as hard as he could, just as soon as I opened the door, he then split just as quick. What a nut!

Yet I could pretty much knead away the pain and sufferings of fights I'd be forced to defend myself in. Sometimes winning, sometimes loosing.

Getting Robbed

Many incidences followed, come what may, one right after another, such as the trucker who picked me up outta Wyoming that ripped off all my shit when he stopped to refuel at a truck stop and I jumped out to use the bathroom. Stealing away everything I owned in that ol' suitcase. Losing even Bears Atlas. While he left me flat with just the clothes on my back.

Now you wanna talk about cold! Some waitress's there would put me up for a few days and help me with a new set of duds.

3rd Real Relationship

Did you know, did I ever tell ya? I was shot by a 22 bullet. I shot myself with a 22 caliber rifle at that, over cough cough cough. spittle gag. Yes. A GUY.

What?! You heard right. A guy man. haha. I was lost in love, and he was gonna leave me because his "Mommy" told him to. I was around 22, maybe 24. He was like a year or 2 older than me. I was sloshed when I did it. I have to admit. A drunk Aileen does me no good. I always "get in trouble."

Well, let me go on to something else.

***

Then my 3rd was in my 20s. Mick Loder, who I shot myself over. Geez! What a waste of time. He joined the Coast Guards and turned fag. Yuck! Hahaha like I've room to talk. I started the gay scene at 28. though there were other guys before 28 off and on in my life I was with for a while. But these 3 were the only ones I 'really loved'.

Oh memories, memories! Even the bad ones. Great experiences. Gave me plenty of wisdom down the silver cord of this life's living in.

***

Shit! I gotta tell ya this one, once upon a time, long ago and far away! Well, there was a girl who was close to me. Like you & I! Nick-nick, we called each other sisters. One night we were in this bar, and she had her purse ripped off. She asked me if I could help her get it back. So I go up to the thief and tap her on the shoulder and told her "alright! My sister here tells me you've got her purse. How about Just given it back, and all will be cool!" She was like a viper, beginning to yell. So we went outside. She had these pointed toes, steal (I believe) tipped cowboy boots on with her 2 piece outfit.

We're standing there, I am mouthing off to her, to just hand over the purse. She kicks me! She does this with all her might and Just miss's my clit by fractions. Hits the lip. I bend over slightly, and immediately straightened up. and said, "that didn't hurt!" And punched her. We're fighting away! They break us up eventually. Ouch!! So the next day. One side of my puss was black, and I mean blackish/blue/black, as well as my leg all the way down to my knee/inside my leg. Talk about lucky!

I bet ya had she of zeroed in on my clit. I wouldn't be able to turn on if I hammered it. Jackhammered. hahaha. Della got her purse back the next day. Incidentally, she also was Max's sister. The guy I shot myself over. So she found it lying in a ditch alongside the road.

Toni – 'My First Lezzy Encounter' (Aged 29)

Beating Up A Homophobe

I've got to tell ya a story about Smart Alex bar & a fight I got into unexpectedly, so you'll know how much I changed, from a teen, when it comes to fighting. This happened around 85.

Well, after I bought Toni, my first lezzy encounter and the girl I'd been living with for a year, a pressure cleaner and all the equipment. Around 4 grand or so was spent. She up and left me. I was so in love with her, her leaving that is, the ripping me off didn't bug me, I just wanted her back, bad!

Around 4 days later, from her up and running, I was hanging out sudsing up all the pain. Now, this bar was a regular of ours. Well, it was around 11 a.m. Things were still slow in the bar, not much of anyone there, we were all kicking back, shooting pool, listening to the jukebox.

Me, I was settled down at the corner bar, resting away with a long neck bottle of bud. Suddenly this guy wearing all this army fatigue jazz walks in. Big guy, around 6'3" and around 275 and decides to order a brew.

Around 10 minutes go by. I'm not paying any attention to him, Just nursing my memories and pain of Toni being gone.

Suddenly. he turns to me and mouths off. "You Look like a lesbian to me." And I said "yeah, and so what if I am?" He said "I'm gonna kick your lezzy fucking ass black and blue all over this bar!" I slammed my beer down, and flew off the bar stool, pushing away the 3 bar stools between him. and I and jumped his ass. I threw him over 2 pool tables that were in the bar. beating him with my fist or standing over him, kicking the fuck out of him. I dragged him off by the arm, and hair, of what little he had, and dragged him to the back of the bar. Now everyone was watching me, cheering me on. "Kick his ass Lee," and so on! I was in the most violent rage you've ever seen.

As I dragged him out the door, and into the dirt, dust started flying everywhere.

Everyone was at the back door watching. I said "if you ever come back to this bar, I'll kill you!" Then Skip cut in, a biker dude, and he said "no! If you ever come back to this bar, we'll kill you! Get outta here!" Needless to say! I got royal respect, then I knew for certain, if I go off, I could whip anyone's ass. I was shocked afterwards myself in other words. Smart Alex bar was a trip anyway. A lot of wild times I had in that bar.

Relationship with Tyria Moore

Trying To 'Tame' Ty Into Looking More Feminine

Boots and a mini skirt? Overkill? Me? Hahaha that's a joke and a half.
What cracks me up is I've seen fat ass Tyria in a dress, in her butch brush
cut hairdo and all. You'd die if you'd seen it. She looks pathetic as hell! I
still love her, but God she's ugly in a dress. And guess who conned her
into shaving her legs. Yes, me! Hahaha when I first met her, I asked her
why her legs were hairy like a man's. She said, "honey cause I'm a
lesbian." How I feel is that if you're gonna be gay. You can still look like a
woman. I got her to grow her head hair semi-long once. But it only lasted
a short while before she cut it all off again like a guy's, brush-cut style,
humph! She was difficult to tame! Haha.

Ty Getting Fired For Handing In Lost Money

I remember when Ty was working at the Laundry Mat back in Daytona,
in the year of either 86 or 87, and wound up finding a whole slew of coins
behind one of the washers. By the time I arrived there. she was wrapping
up the last roll of 125 bucks. So since no buddy knew it ever was back
there, I thought for sure, that day I could take off and not have to hustle
then. Yet, low and behold and one of the reasons I loved her so – was for

her down-to-earth ways and honesty, she gave all the quarters back to the Managers. And mind you – we were flat outta food and behind in rent. Days away that we also wouldn't know – from being evicted. And then of all things. Regardless of that act of kindness which she did in all honesty, was fired by the managers in claims of 'stealing from them,' I couldn't believe it. She was a good honest worker. While I think they fired her because of 2 things. We were lesbians, and she would smoke pot in the place once in a while. As I kept telling her it was a bad idea. Yet she'd do it anyhow. So. Erm. Erm. Erm. Too bad Ay?!

These Shoes Were Made For Walking

My shoes? Well, buddy, those babies didn't walk as many miles as the ones I threw away. Dick Mills who I met and stayed with for only 4 days, had bought those for his girlfriend. I was in need of shoes real bad, he first decided to give them to me cause he & his girlfriend broke up. Then as I was about to leave his place he changed his mind. So I ripped them off. Hahaha. So there are not many miles on them.

Now the ones I threw out! They had some royal miles put on them! 1,000s! All of Florida was my turf, so the ones I threw out were ragged and torn royal. You're probably thinking why didn't you get a new pair? Well, because I was too busy hustling and too lazy too.

Just eat – work – party – sleep. I didn't much care about anything else. Only Tyria's happiness and stuff for her. When she had to split, well, then I really didn't care about anything! At all! Needless to say, life sucks. You find yourself true love and happiness, then eventually it slips away. The world is a wasted place. Lucifer has caused it to serve no purpose. And that's why my friend I cant wait to be where Christ is, where life there is all full of meaning.

Love Her Forever

You lucky babe! You got to see Dateline. But not I. Boy was I pissed. About me, and couldn't even see it. So I have no idea, what it had. Was anything edited, did they chop, distort? I hope you're right, that I did OK.

Knowing me, I'm not very photogenic, so I probably was pretty funky looking.

How did Tyria look? Dorky I bet! She's not a good looker. But oh did we ever party, and do most everything together. I still love her. Can't let her go! She could shoot me, and if I survived it I would've had open arms, still, with lots of love to give. That's just the way I am. I love to give love. I know I've hurt myself over being this away. But the pain doesn't feel so bad when you know you're struggling to give love, for a cause that really pays off.

I know for a fact Ty and I would've stayed together for life. If this shit had never have happened. She told me on the phone, in one of the recorded phone calls at VCBJ. Lord did I cry on that phone. Cut me up like a machete attack to the heart. Arlene wants to keep her away from my funeral. I want Tyria at my funeral more than anything. I'll die thinking of her, as well as you. I don't believe much thought of anyone else will come to mind.

Abusing Ty & Their Pets

Man, Dawn I kid you not. You and I are alike. I love animals so bad. The animal can be as ugly as Tyria, and I'd still love the dickens out of it. hahaha! Once Tyria kicked Maggie. Wrong, we nearly came close to a knock-out drag-out. Then I once witnessed her on a drunk throw Tyler against a wall. Another Wrong move! Lord, we nearly tore into each other on that one too. I hate Animal abuse as much as abuse of women.

Too bad society has me all wrong, from all the cop lies and defamation put out on me. Because really I was all "Love". Now I'm not. Too angry from the whole mess. Even at myself! But before my arrest, and before things got hairy. I was nothing but full of "Love".

Whew! I got on a roll, didn't I? From loving animals to, animal abuse, then side-tracked off onto the deranged system. oh well! Forgive me if I began to bore you. Feels good to get it off my chest at times. Love Lee

***

I'm reading about your cats. Right on! They're so precious. I felt like the beast-master with my critters. Dusty one day was watching me flush the toilet. Well as the water was swirling away going down / he jumped on the seat to watch in amazement. Then to my amazement, he started pawing the flusher until it worked. It flushed, he watched again it swirl down. From then on, he'd go in there and do it now and then. Flush the toilet.! God I loved that cat. And all my kids (critters).

It breaks my heart flashing back in memory and seeing how I did neglect their health. Then, I didn't know it! But now I do, I was carrying on one blind, wild, life.

Feeling Manipulated By Toni & Ty

Let's get some bread off her, the fame she has won. Myself I hadn't that planned. The cops did that one. Just for their own crooked-ass fabricated movie they're working on. With no other than my ex-lover. She's lying through her ass that it wasn't self-defense. Cause she's been promised by the cops hundreds of thousands of dollars, and no matter how much I loved her and showed it to her, she's willing to take me down, for the almighty dollar.

Ironically, I still love her too. That's because of all the memories of all the good times we shared together.

Toni + Tyria were both materialistic and money-hungry to the core. This is one of the major fights we'd always get into. This is the royal mistake I made by her wishes, I had enough regulars to get by, but do you think Tyria cared? Hell no! She'd ask me to still go out! So, I was in love. She had me easily manipulated. Yeah! I was a fool. Such a waste. Wish I never would have met her.

Hurting Over Break Up Letters

Ty sent me 2 flicks of herself with new front choppers in. Man, what an improvement. She looks really different now, in a really good way. Amazing what 2 front teeth can do for real! She's really hurting over our breakup in all of this. I can tell with her letters. I am too, but I'm trying to hide it from her, so she won't hurt as much. I tell you, I love her so deeply. Like you. These feelings are more 'sisterly', like our friendship. For I swear, I now am totally against lesbianism. It's a 'royal' strike against God and his laws of nature. So I've tossed any sick ideas like these, way out the window. But I really love her 'bad' as a sisterly image thing.

Ty Sent Her A Fancy Gold Watch

I received Ty's package. Aw! The sweetheart picked out a real cool-looking watch. It's got these roman numerals around the gold ring of the watch's outer cover, has a gold hand on it, one for minutes moving around and its backdrop face of it is marble looking. Green streaks like a tiger look. Cool!

Letting Go Of Ties To Ty & Lori

I see you've finally got in touch with ties to Ty. I guess she'd prefer to let things go too. I'm just glad to hear through her mom that she's doing good and working a lot. She loves to work because she loves people. It helps her to socialize and create friends. By now she has dozens and they've helped her get over me! All of which makes me that much happier. I know she's doing well and is fine. so I'll leave it at that I guess. And so if you would. Go ahead and quit calling. Don't want to piss her off. And please do the same with Lori.

Living the good life

Staying with Carnies For 6 Weeks In Florida

Good Morning! And hows thee ol' hippy doing?! Good, Good, Good, Good, Good I hope. Ay! There's a new song out I'm blown away in love with. It's been out for some time now but I'd forgotten to mention it to ya. You can add this one to funeral songs if you'd like. It's called Carnival by Natalie Merchant, cool tune.

Ty and I met some carnies in Homosassa Florida from Illinois. Hip chicks, boy. This song reminds me of them and their carnie stories, plus I just love the cut. These gals lived in a 20 ft trailer – had a 6 axle truck to pull it with, and traveled all over America with the carnies – as vendors and game hosts for. What was extraordinary about them is the animals that traveled with them. Let's see if I can remember all their pets! They had a Turtle – Couple of – Couple of Parrots – Finches – around 3 or 4 cats – 3 dogs – a snake – a hamster. And all these animals traveled all around Buddy with their chicks in that 20 ft. trailer. We were amazed! All the critters looked – well-groomed, well-fed, quite happy! But how they acted up in the trailer while under tow of traveling is beyond me. I'm sure it swayed along the highway hahaha.

The girls made good in the business. Anywhere from 700 to 1500 a week. Yep! A week! They kept telling Ty and me, if we'd set up some wheels, we could hook up our 18 ft trailer and follow em up to the main office in Indiana, they'd teach us the carnie life and lead us into the business where we could make out as they were at 700 to 1500 a week. Of course, we never did get the wheels we needed and they rolled on up north some 6 weeks later. This was in 87. Cool chicks. And from the stories of their carnival life, so were the carnies they worked with.

Getting Drunk At The Beach

What's this! a Recliner! Oh Lordy. one of my favorites. May you have heavenly days of comfort in it. I remember the recliner I once had. Back when I lived on Silver-beach on A1A and Daytona. That recliner was my pride and joy. After work, I'd whip up some boozing and flick on the stereo, laid back listening in the recliner, and bingo. I was gone, Drunk and happy and crashing in that big ol' hug of a chair. So my dearly beloved buddy. May you rest peacefully in yours. Sleep-in's a breeze in one too.

Cycle Adventures To The Beach

Hi there! Bicycle riding, how cool! I used to do it all the time. Use to ride 29 miles to Flagler from Daytona and back, like every other day. I'm glad ta hear you're getting into some real exercise. In my early 20s on days off from work, I'd pack 4 mellow yellows on it, with a beach towel wrapped around the handlebars, with bungee cord and a Bible. That was it. Except for me, dressed in Ts and shorts with a bathing suit underneath. Eventually, I'd strip down to just my bathing suit, and cruise out to Flagler. Then once out there at a beach area so deserted from any walking life. I'd hang out and read the Bible, as the beautiful ocean's shore of waves crashed in, making the most sublime tranquil sounds. Just reading and laying out, God, and the heaven-lies with Christ was always on my mind. Ty went with me once. Had a ball. Most of the time she was working though. And a lot of times I cruised out there on a 12 speed just to ditch my bike out in the woods and hit the freeway for the day, hooking around, then dropped off near where my bike was, and cruise back. It was relaxing to my nerves. Before I went and after I'd be done for the day tricking around. And check this out. Never bought any new tires for it. And never had a flat. I knew God was holding those tires together. And I was glad. 'Ding, Ding, Ding! Look out! I'm coming through hahaha.' Love Aileen

Sunbathing & Treasure Hunting

Needless to say, besides rock, I also love tropical-sounding music. Reminds me of the Keys when I lived out there.

There I was every day when I first arrived – lying out under the bridge of US 1 and near the Oceans 80(s) motel resort. Oil all over me, black bikini on – and binoculars. Radio jamming as I'd pass the Sunny day of ray soaking with imaginable thoughts of Pirates aboard ships a sail at sea or Treasure's of many lost in. And I'd take the binoculars. and walk out waste deep in the water, then set my binoculars. in it as well, checking out the oceans floor, hoping like hell, I'd just get lucky and find an old Spanish coin – as I was. hahaha.

Crazy?! Oh well, this is how I kicked back and tried enjoying every breath I took out there in this tropical coral reef (tail end) of Florida. And now here I sit some 100 miles from (on) Death Row. Life.! It's so strange at times. Isn't it? Never know what that future will hold in store. Geez!

Life Philosophy

Convincing Ty it was a good idea to give money to the homeless, what comes around goes around.

Darn, Darn, Darn, Sure wish you and I could go shopping together. Ty and I had a lot of fun. No doubt. She's got some good memories for sure. I loved also helping out vagrants, and downright nasty-looking homeless people. I'd pull bills out all the time and just be charitable to them. Ty didn't like this too much because I'd give 5s or 10s sometimes. And it could be when we spent most of our money already, and just a little bit left for the end of the day to party on. But I'd always look at her and say, Ty, what comes around goes around. Someday! We could be rewarded by God with a fortune for doing this. Like winning the lotto.

And you know, We almost won. I missed by 1 number. We won 34500 bucks for 4 numbers right. And hair missed $275,995, big Ones.

And as we came this close, I'd then always say to her. See, see, see! You never know! God will repay you for your charity. Ty would say, Yeah, but what if they just buy drugs or booze with it. Then, I'd always say "so? That's between them and God. I'm only doing my part between God and me. What they do afterward, is their business between themselves and him. Besides! They very well may not be either." And Ty finally started seeing what I was saying and would give too.

Living Modestly

I received 7 letters from ya this week. Whew! Sad stuff. I've been through it all like you. So I know exactly how you feel! When you go through stuff like this you learn to understand yourself needing to accept a more poverty-stricken way of living, for your future to become prosperous again. Like I say, today to dream of nice things, to have and hold for years ahead is fruitless to do.

Because of the way our world conditions are. There's too much chaos, and economic downfalls, to have one hope for bigger and better things, on an income tight and cannot be played with. "Hoping it will all fall in place," to be afforded. But can't be. That's why myself if I were free, I'd be seeking a place, that may be a dive to live in, and searching more into saving all extra funds after rent. Which would be dirt cheap to later start all over again.

From all my roller coaster rides. I've learned that, if you accept poverty, humble yourself, and not let it hurt your pride. Pocket-it. You'll go a much longer way. As you know I turned to hooking to beat the warrants. I learned also, that I could survive like normal middle-class people's wages. Instead of like Ty's, which was $300 every 2 weeks. $600 a month. Give me a break! Our rent alone was $385 a month. Electric was around $90 a month in the summer and $190 a month in the winter. Plus food $70 to $100 a week. How in the hell do they expect anyone to live off of $4.25 an hour.

Eventually, people get pissed off. No wonder they have crime and of the ugliest kind today. People's heads are getting messed up.

I'm really sorry to hear you lost your house, Dawn. But if you look at all I've said. You later in the future may be glad you have. For you may own outright, use your head. Don't let yourself go through this again. Please. For now.

One Reason For Carrying The Gun That Would Later Be Used In The Murders

When I met Toni & Ty, I learned an excellent remedy for preventing getting IDs or cash stolen. 'Wear a wallet.' Chuckle, Chuckle. So purses went out the window. It worked well also on the road hooking. If any guy rode off with my purse & duffle bag while in a store getting a beer, or taking a piss, he'd get shit. When I got the gun, then my bag went into the store with me. And so this is how I kept my funds and ID and my protection safe from being stolen. Good idea Ay?!

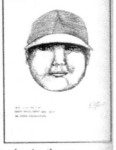

Composite sketches of women seen leaving the car
belonging to the missionary, Peter Siems, July 4, 1990.

Last Relationship, On The Run After The Murders

Nick Broomfield Interview

Nick voice-over: In loneliness and desperation Aileen ended up with this man called Dick Mills.

Dick: This is the paper right here?

Nick: Yeah it's called "MY SEX ROMPS WITH KINKY MAN KILLER".

Nick voice-over: Dick had sold his story to the news of the world.

Dick Mills: All I want to know is, who's the best lawyer out there to sue them for this trash. I never talked that shit.

Nick: Can I quote you for a bit to see if you said this stuff? "We were lying in bed one night for a bit when she started talking about her favorite sexual fantasies, she said she often got turned on by imagining she had a black hood over her head and tied to a tree in the forest, then a guy would come up, rape her, then shoot her in the head, she said the actual killing would make her climax, I was real sickened by what she said."

Dick Mills: Wrong, wrong, there's partial truth to that, but most of that I don't know where it came from, or who got it, or nothing about it. And you can check any film anywhere in the country, who's got it and I never said that. OK, it goes along the lines of... she told me one time, that the idea was she'd like to lay in bed out there somewhere in the forest, the woods or I don't know, the mountains or something, have a hood over her head and someone would crawl in through the window and... no, they had their hood on or something, then would rape her or this and that kinda shit, and she liked that, but as far as all these other things go pertaining to... there's no reality to it.

Nick: Did you get any idea that she hated men? Or...?

Dick Mills: No, I just got the feeling she was a dyke, which is what she was, but I didn't know she was a killer, there was no way I could know that.

Nick: I mean could you have known that when you made love to her or...?

Dick Mills: Nah, not particularly, she probably just liked it either way, whatever came along, didn't really seem to matter much, it was just another bad experience I'm sure for both of us.

Tampa Bay Times Article

A former lover of Aileen Wuornos, the woman accused of slaying several middle-aged motorists in Central Florida, describes her as a "wild, savage party animal" with a voracious appetite for sex and booze. Dick Mills said he met Ms. Wuornos in Wet Willie's, a biker bar in Daytona Beach, in December 1990 after he separated from his wife, Connie. He said the meeting sparked a five-day affair with Ms. Wuornos, who told him her name was Lee Green.

"There's only two people I've ever met who have met the devil and shaken his hand. One is me. The other is her," Mills, a 45-year-old Vietnam Veteran, told the Ocala Star-Banner.

Ms. Wuornos, he said, was devastated over the recent breakup of a five-year relationship with Tyria Moore.

Mills said Ms. Wuornos would drink heavily and weep uncontrollably while crying out for Ms. Moore. He said he and Ms. Wuornos were attracted to each other because both were depressed about separating from their partners.

Court records show Ms. Moore told authorities that Ms. Wuornos told her in December that she had "killed a guy."

Ms. Moore is in protective custody in an undisclosed area and is expected to testify against Ms. Wuornos, who is being held without bond pending a murder trial scheduled in September.

Mills said Ms. Wuornos, 34, "hated the cops" and "went wild when she saw one."

Mills took Ms. Wuornos to a family gathering. His family members found her aggressive and obnoxious and eventually asked Mills to take her away.

"My impression was that she was a hippie who never made it out of the '60s," said Tammy Sibbernsen, Mills' daughter.

Mills appears flippant about his involvement with Wuornos. "Hell, it's a party man. You only go around once," he said.

Final Words On Her Past

I was thinking, I bet Dawn always says to herself, 'God Ty sure was ugly, she wasn't that great looking, so what did she see in her?' Chuckle. Chuckle.

It was basically because she was sooooo sweet. 90% of her whole behavior was just super sweet and innocent, regardless that she preferred a gay life. I wanted to just reach out and hug her all the time. Just every minute if I could! Yet it was all in a "sisterly sense" with no interest in the sex part. No way. It was to against the grain of nature for me and God. So all my love leaned more towards just pure friendship, extraordinarily tight.

And then of course my magnified love for her had me more careful than ever before out there thumbing, just to keep myself in one piece for her. God only knew when I'd see Ty again should I have been busted. So I decided to rip off a gun and risk carrying it 'regardless', as I lugged it around in a tote bag for at least 3 months before reaching up with Richard Mallory.

And then Ty and I were running into problems too. People kept messing with us just because we were gay. While landlords wound up kicking us out continually.

Then we had other problems, be it with our pets! Having acquired in all our 4½ years together 3 cats and a dog. Eventually to wind up with only one cat in the end that some guys next door I know kidnapped to kill, only because they found out we were gay. A gay couple living together. So messing with my beloved pets who were like kids to me also fueled the fire within.

And as we moved from "Rutland Florida" to Ocean Views RV. resort there in Ormond Beach just above Daytona, we bumped into another situation 'because we were gay'. Only then to be told that we were too loud and so had to move out in 24 hours. Our 18 ft. corsair trailer that we wound up with from Homosassa for $1,500 and a mere 50 bucks a month in payments for.

Then Ty landed a job as a laundry worker for a Motel called Casa Del Mar only to make $300 every 2 weeks. We then moved just a mile down from the park to a motel that'd accept pets, only for the bills to skyrocket from $150 a month to $140 a week.

Only to run into another problem. As it was that every time we went to work, the animals made a mess of the place and a hell of a lot of a racket. Knowing we were surely gonna get evicted for it and did, I headed back out doing the usual, yet knowing now I'd have to make a hell of a lot more than ever before! Like $1,500 in 3 days, and that just wasn't going to happen unless clients got rolled.

Then to top things off, we were now in the rainy season! I could only make about $80 a day whenever it did. When on any other given day of a sunny one I could make $150 to $300. So, I told Ty I'd head South and hopefully pull out of it all from down there. Only for me to be back the same day and let her know it was falling everywhere!

So needless to say, we were really in a fix. I knew for certain I'd wind up rolling a client. So headed back on out to spend a couple of days down in Fort Myers, hopefully, then I'd beat the rain and not have to jack one.

And then there was another usual problem I had, which was missing Ty every time I went off to hook. Missing her by the end of every day, and just had to get back. So this occurred by the second day that I stayed over in Fort Myers, therefore with that, decided then to head back regardless that I'd wind up stuck thumbing through the night. Knowing the risk in doing so of one of either two things possibly happening. Be that of it either hard for me to get a ride, or just flat run into trouble. All of which is why in my 5½ years of hooking, I only worked from sun up to sundown. Did then and started heading back to Ty, when Richard Mallory picked me up around 10:30 at night on the I-4.

And so I'll end it there. Not willing to go any further into any more details, that on 7 different occasions while I thumbed and hooked, we were left in another financial upset, and with the rain still coming down hard, I robbed and killed 7, in the year of 1990.

Aileen C. Wuornos

2001

Pictures

Dawn Botkins and the walnut tree she planted in Wuornos's memory
where Aileen's ashes are scattered.

Redheaded like Leo Pittman, the father Aileen never met, Tyria Jolene Moore became the big love of Aileen Wuornos's life—and a fellow suspect in the string of Florida murders.

Keith Wuornos with his father/grandfather, Lauri Wuornos, on a family trip.

Aileen and Keith with Britta Wuornos, the grandmother who raised them as if they were her own children, on vacation two years before Britta's death.

Britta Wuornos, the same day.

Aileen and Keith's childhood friend Mark Fearn stands at the site where Aileen built the first of many forts in the woods close to her home.

The Wuornos home, above. Nearby neighbors heard Aileen's cries when her grandfather punished her.

What was once the Wuornos home in Troy, Michigan. Above the front door is one of the two windows from which Aileen regularly made her late-night escapes.

The flat, deserted roads amidst the dense central Florida woods where Lee took her prostitution clients...and, on her killing days, her robbery and murder victims.

One of the trailer homes that Lee and Ty lived in at Homossassa Springs, in 1989. Reminiscent of her childhood home, the trailer's windows were kept covered by Lee. Lee and Ty practiced shooting at trees and beer cans in the barren park.

Wet Willie's Tavern in a seedy stretch of the Daytona, Florida, area. One of Lee's many pool-playing and drinking hangouts.

The shrine that has been erected to Lee Wuornos outside the back of the Last Resort Bar where she was finally arrested by investigator, Larry Horzepa, on January 9, 1991.

Former Marion County Sheriff's Office investigator Brian Jarvis outside The Last Resort Bar in Port Orange, Florida, in 2008. Photograph by David Taylor.

The entrance to The Last Resort Bar, where Aileen was playing pool shortly before her arrest. Photograph by David Taylor.

A heap of "dead motorcycles" outside The Last Resort Bar. Photograph by David Taylor.

The Last Resort Bar advertises its proud slogan on its trailer/truck. Photograph by David Taylor.

The intersection between Florida's SR 90 and the I-75 highway. Desolate stretches of the I-75 highway were favorite hitchhiking spots for Aileen. Photograph by David Taylor.

After murdering Charles Richard "Dick" Humphreys, Aileen Wuornos cleaned out his car at US 27 and Boggy Marsh Creek Road so she couldn't be identified. Photograph by David Taylor.

Victim Dick Humphreys' car was found behind this abandoned gas station at the SR 90 and I-75 interchange in Suwannee County, Florida. Photograph by David Taylor.

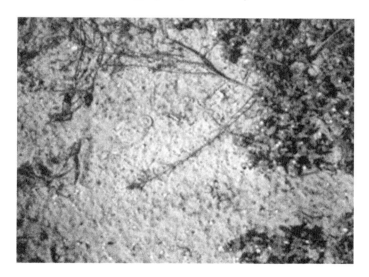

Look closely and you'll see the spent .22 caliber shell casing in the soil that was positively linked to Aileen Wuornos's gun. Photograph by David Taylor.

Room 8 at the former Fairview Motel—now called The Scoot Inn—where Aileen Wuornos and Tyria Moore used to stay. Photograph by David Taylor.

The former Fairview Motel. Photograph by David Taylor.

The former Fairview Motel. Photograph by David Taylor.

The old Fairview Motel sign lends a touch of nostalgia in 2013 to the motel once frequented by Aileen Wuornos and Tyria Moore. Photograph by Jackelyn Giroux.

Movie producer Jackelyn Giroux signed up the rights to Aileen Wuornos's life story soon after her arrest. In 2013, the film-maker revisited Aileen's old haunt The Fairview Motel in its new, spruced-up incarnation as The Scoot Inn. Photograph by Jackelyn Giroux.

One of Aileen's letters, with her signature emphasis & emojis:

Aileen Wuornos
A150924   DR #4
Broward Correctional Institution
P.O. Box 84-8540
Pembroke Pines Florida
        33084   1-15-96

        Dear Dawn,

            I thought I'd be writting another letter the same day when I
said I'd move on to another one "today" in my last letter. But! Low : Behold
I whipped out the Bible and became highly engrossed in study. So forgive
me my dear. These kinda things (is) intrigue do happen to me, when- "Ever"
I open the Good Book.
            Wrote your Mom yesterday. Wishin her a Happy Valentines
and gettin lost in the Lord with her. Your Mom is one Beautiful Women
and the fond memories I have, having met her during our kids days
are sentimental to the photogenic pass within my mind. Wonderful Lady
and so was your Dad. Besides cool headed Ducky. 😊 — 👑 treat
                                                                              them all.
            I notice my writting still is a bit tense around the edges
of movement accross the page. Guess this is due to alot a lack of
exercise. Ha Ha Ha! But my wrist doesnt hurt - nor the joints of
my fingers since I've been being "Very Careful" at just what to eat off
the prison food trays. No great loss. The food is horribal - at times
anyway! Chuckle. ehhhhhh. Bluuuu. Ok.
            Wow, was watchin "Real Ghost III" on 33 the other
day. Yikes - Scavery as shit. There real stories of Ghost encounters.
Good . . . Halloween stuff! Better than Freddy cougar - Man!
Needless to say - Its basically demon possession that causes such
encounters - Be they ones that are vicious as hell itself. But I've
been really pondering in thought to these good encounters . wheather
to believe they happened (or) was it another trick in the bag by Lucifer

against the mourning families. You see - the problem I'm having to believe these spirits could be christians passed on, but come back to let them know there (is) life after death. And any séances etc of spirit contact. Is that. . . . No one yet has expressed in there out of body new demensional existence - whats out there! whats on thee other side! "Only near death experiences have." But not the dead in contact with the living. They only say they miss them and are sorry for any bad vibes they may of laid on one another while they were alive. So I'm lost in just what to believe on this paranormal jazzy. But it was - Extremely interesting - to watch.

& Phyllis still hasn't written. Wonder just whats up her sleeve now. You know - the Pre-med strategies - then contact. Only on a norm - these type when they Pre-med its for some bound by the world evil purpose. Hum. I'm lost about her now. 4-sure!

You were saying here in response to me feeling that if I died right now- I'd probably go to hell. And you feeling here for a surety I wouldn't. Well all I can say to this once again to make you better understand my meaning - is - In the privacy of my cell and my mind.., Grosses Hatred has possessed me to the max..! I could be Lucifers Sister in retrospects to my life lead and the hell I'm in now. With of-course all the injustice regardless that the fact is true - I did Kill 7 men. This! my dear Buddy! causes me to cuss in the evilest way "to Myself." . . . and hate Everything nearly "to Myself." I cannot die like this. For the Spirit of God "WILL NOT DWELL (NOR) SEAL SUCH A SOUL ...!" And now that I do know Gods word and God in general. I must change (or else) upon death face the facts. of such a person who continues to be ██████ wantingly lead into the fallen state, shall only reap what they sow. Good seed can only change the inner Man. A Bad seed can only deteriorate further into Darkness. So the inner Man must FORCE oneself to change all the corrupt area's of Flesh and Soul. Or forget Redemption. Forget Salvation. For the spirit of God is pure, and will only abide in the house and temple of a soul who "Sincerely" only seeks to (as well) be. A deep seated desire must take in effect. So this is the gross Tarnished area's I must change. Itee take time, but the me I am now - and from the past - must shed. It has been - exceedingly wicked - plus by my tongue and thoughts even behind these four walls - still is. I must push evil of any kind I have been conditioned in throughout some 25-30 years imbedded too - by cultural and traditional influences. Besides the great many other sins I practiced into, / and rid them. Become a New Being! a new creature! When you do - The Past must completely - go - Bye Bye. All the wicked things - and tongue - and all. Good Memories are fine. Clean and Decent ones - A-OK. But the other left overs that trained you to walk in evil Blind or not. Must Go! This my friend is what I'm working on and trying to Master. Words must become pure - thoughts must become pure - the act must be cleaned up! And while it is - Love must come back in. And ALL hatred and Malice must be forgive and forgotten. If others dont forgive you. So what. As long as your inner-self honestly does others, the record then of yours's becomes sinless in this area. It will show that you "Always" forgave - Regardless what came your way - And in all "True Sincerity." And so this my friend - is what I mean about - if I died today I'd probably go straight to hell. For all that is in me - is still old and evil. It must change.

Yoo Dawn! Can I borrow your juices. Eow. The stuff your

creation with that thing around. Scrumptions. Emm. ☺ OK...As
whats some of the other's you've juiced up. Ought to drum up some
labels to your concoctions. Ha Ha Ha. Dont forget to note down
what ya did. You may hit on something to pass on for generations to
come. A Block Buster idea.! 😊 Like WoW. Dig it Man, look
what I drummed up. Where's... Heloise. See he rich !!!
He Ha Ha 👑 You could Publish a little booklet entitled.
Dawn Botkins Homemade Juicers. Zinch to blend. 25 recipes.
Aileen I've already went through 25 concoctions.! 🌿 What!?
If you have you must be Water-logged. Peeing must be hell on ya.
Ha Ha Ha Ha .....

Well. Its gettin close to noon around here. Lunch and Rec.
Will be on the next agenda. So guess I'll close er up here and get
ready for some munchies - then a stoogie. Ha Ha. I wish they
sold cigars. I use to smoke the thin cherry ▇ flavored ones. Emmm.
I always enjoyed the smell of cigars to. AhhHHh 💨 Refreshing!
OK, I'm outta here.

   See ya soon my friend,
    Love ya with all my heart.

      Untill the next Kite
      flys in.

      Squeeze the Veggies !
      Oops I mean Fruit.

      Love
      Aileen,

The Eagle Has Landed. Ink drawing by Aileen Wuornos. Image courtesy of Amber Hogue:

Moon Eagle Valley Ranch. Ink drawing by Aileen Wuornos. Image courtesy of Dave Botkins:

Beam Me Up, Scotty. Ink drawing by Aileen Wuornos. Image courtesy of
Amber Hogue:

Midnight Blue. Ink drawing by Aileen Wuornos. Image courtesy of Dave Botkins:

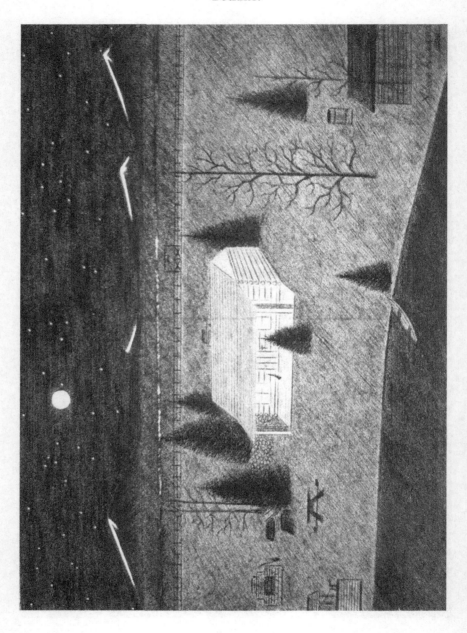

Shadows Pine Ridge Resort. Ink drawing by Aileen Wuornos. Image courtesy of Dave Botkins:

Acknowledgments

Lisa Kester   *&*   *Daphne Gottlieb*

Quoting from the Dear Dawn book as this is a continuation of their work, whose editors were Lisa Kester and Daphne Gottlieb:

> The editors would like to thank Anne Horowitz for her tireless, brilliant, and ruthless editing; this book would not be here without her hard work. Words are insufficient to express the depth of our gratitude.
>
> Lisa would like to express her sincere gratitude to Daphne Gottlieb for her enormous gift of dedication and focus on this book. She has been the anchor in this project from day one.
>
> A special thanks goes to Jesse Merril, for enlisting us in this project. Without her gentle nudge, this project would not have been started. Also, heartfelt gratitude goes to Brenda Bass, for believing in this project from the start and helping to make it happen.
>
> Thanks to Susan Seager and Jonathan Gottlieb, who had wisdom when we needed it. Thanks to our agent Katie Boyle, who was there when we needed her.

Thanks to Aja Aguirre, Meg Chilton, Deborah Teramis Christian, Annalee Cobbett, Joie Rey Cohen, Amber Hogue, Cassidy Jones, Marie Militana, Cat Ondriezek, and Jae Sevilus for inputting assistance and various other supports.

Most of all, thanks to Dawn and Dave Botkins. Dave did a great deal of preparation for this project by scanning and organizing the letters and photographs. Dawn has courageously opened her letter file and her heart to us and made this all possible.

Printed in Great Britain
by Amazon